Praise for *Mentor Like Jesus*

Regi Campbell is a gift to leaders; especially those that want to make a real difference and leave a lasting legacy. *Mentor Like Jesus* is packed full of vision and practical helps for investing your life in others. But what makes it so different is not that it's small group friendly, but that it's small group dependent. It's a helpful mentoring strategy for any small group ministry.

Bill Willits
Director of Group Life
North Point Community Church

Regi Campbell is a wise man of God and when he talks, I listen. I have watched him have an incredible impact on many young men in the Atlanta area through his mentoring process; and finally he has put to paper the principles that he uses that were modeled after Christ's own methods. This is the best mentoring book I have read and I highly recommend it to anyone who feels a nudge or calling to mentor others; or to those who want to be mentored.

Joel Manby
President and CEO
Herschend Family Entertainment

Mentor Like Jesus is Regi's best yet and a powerful reminder of God's call to live as a discipling leader who is bearing much fruit. This is the best I've seen yet on how to live out the responsibility of making disciples of Jesus Christ in an intentional way. Be prepared to be challenged to pay it forward and to be motivated to get in the game in your important role as a mentoring leader.

Steve Wood
Senior Pastor
Mount Pisgah United Methodist Church

I was new to mentoring a year ago and now I'm sold-out. Investing in the next generation of Christian leaders is the best use of my time. They are hungry to learn from my successes, my failures and my lessons learned. Next Generation Mentoring provided me the tools I needed to be an effective mentor right from the start.

Charlie Paparelli
President of Paparelli Ventures
Chairman of High Tech Ministries

I've never heard of a more meaningful mentoring ministry than the one Regi Campbell practices. So many young men in our church have been the direct beneficiaries of someone who seeks to mentor like Jesus. I hope this insight by Regi will challenge many—especially those in the Boomer Generation—to the really great opportunity of mentoring the next generation.

G. Bryant Wright
Senior Pastor
Johnson Ferry Baptist Church

One of the biggest challenges for young leaders is their inability to recognize what they don't know. Regi's relational approach to trans-generational mentoring solves this ignorance gap through the practical work of life on life mentoring.

Gabe Lyons
Founder—Fermi Project
Coauthor of *unChristian: What a New Generation Really Thinks about Christianity*

In the manner that Jesus' mentoring ministry turned "regular" fisherman and tax collectors into apostles, so Regi Campbell's mentoring ministry has turned "regular" business people into disciples and evangelists. I have seen the results and have firsthand knowledge of people who will spend an eternity with Jesus because they were reached by the mentors developed through the program described in *Mentor Like Jesus*.

Price Harding
Founding Partner
CarterBaldwin Executive Search Services

MENTOR
LIKE JESUS

MENTOR
LIKE JESUS

REGI CAMPBELL
WITH RICHARD CHANCY

PUBLISHING GROUP
Nashville, Tennessee

CONTENTS

ACKNOWLEDGMENTS

There isn't a close second when it comes to my biggest champion and cheerleader. Miriam, you're the love of my life, and your support through this writing effort is just like everything else you've done for me—unselfish and empowering. You're the best!

I have to give credit to my kids, Ross and Erin. If wisdom comes from experience, and experience comes from mistakes, then you guys were the victims of a lot of my learning. Thanks for hanging in there with me. I'm proud of you!

While this is my first book with B&H Publishing, I can already tell that Tom Walters, Kim Stanford, Craig Featherstone, Julie Gwinn, and John Thompson are going to be great team members. Thanks for all you do for him!

And importantly, I want to acknowledge the "guinea pigs" who have taught me what I've learned about mentoring. These are the men who have been my mentorees. Most have been through one of my groups, but there are a few with whom I connected long before next-generation mentoring groups came into existence. Thanks for inviting me into your lives and for helping me learn what mentoring is all about.

Brett Smith	Tim Oakley	Cobb Quarles	Jimmy Patton
Eric Bruton	Maury Davis	Bill Chapman	Ross Campbell
Matt Grose	Michael Burton	Dan Guinaugh	Chris Bentson
Scott Chatham	Pete Vekselman	David Clapp	Craig Chapin
Woody Long	Chet Burge	David Hoyt	David Pyle
Pete Loescher	Geoff Tanner	Kevin Harris	Mark Childress
Toby Anderson	Chris Hornsby	Jason Young	Patrick Donovan
Jake Sexton	Chris Woodruff	James Williamson	Adam Fuller
Deepak Shenoy	Clay Shapiro	Dayne Pryor	J. D. Crowe
John Wichman	Neil Stamper	Jonathan Phillipsen	Stephen Loftin
Michael Breed	George "GB" Pratt	J. D. Espana	Todd Cardes
Chris Arias	Brady Holcomb	Justin Zimmerman	Thomas Casson
Rick Steele	Andrew Wright	Nathan May	Larry Hornsby
Scott McDonald	Darrin Starr	Brian Purcell	Steve Rollins
Sean Fennelly	Steve Kemp	Doug Scott	Bryan Miles
Marc Jackson	Jay Overstreet	Jonathan Johnson	Richard Chancy
Mike McGraw	Jeff Sholen	Clay Scroggins	Ed Nolan
Andy Roberts	Sueng Hwan Kang	Dave Katz	Mark Bowling
Brad Belcher			

Thanks guys. Now go and do likewise.

FOREWORD

About ten years ago a man named Regi Campbell came into my life. As with a lot of my friends, we first connected through church. Regi is several years older than me and has had much success in helping "startup" businesses and ministries. I found him to have a lot of wisdom. So as time went on and as our friendship grew, I found that he was a mentor . . . a natural born mentor.

In 2000 Regi handpicked eight young men whom he believed to have a lot of potential. He invited them to his home and told them he'd meet with them three hours each month for a year if they'd show up for every meeting and be there on time. He'd be totally open and transparent with them . . . telling them everything about his successes and his failures. His personal life . . . his business life . . . relationships . . . no holds bared. He would share the books he'd read with them . . . he'd have them memorize Scriptures that had helped him in his walk, . . . but they'd all have to agree from the outset that at some point in the future, when they were ready, they would "pay it forward" and invest in eight younger men just as Regi had.

Turn the clock forward to 2009, and Regi has just "graduated" his eighth group. He's now mentored sixty-four high potential men who are committed to mentoring again . . . and again.

The results have been profound. "Graduates" have become elders in the church, small group leaders, and significant givers. Their wives say they've become better husbands and fathers. A few men have gone into the group "foggy" about their faith and come out knowing for sure they are Christians.

Several months ago I ran into Regi and he was beaming. "Andy, you know about my mentoring deal. Guess what I figured out? I'm just doing what Jesus did!"

Regi has distilled eleven practices Jesus used in mentoring His disciples into the book that you are now holding. As you dig into *Mentor Like Jesus*, you're going to be stunned by the simplicity of Jesus' model.

As Regi shared recently, "My goal is five generations of multiplication. If that happens, more than one million men will have been equipped to manage life better."

But *Mentor Like Jesus* is not just about life skills. As you are about to discover, Regi Campbell is a sold-out follower of Jesus Christ. His passion for mentoring is driven by a desire to teach "up-and-coming" leaders how to integrate their personal faith into every facet of life, including the marketplace.

For this reason Regi has found support for this unique approach to mentoring in several of Atlanta's leading churches. *Mentor Like Jesus* was not designed as a church program . . . that may come later. Nevertheless, church leaders are enthusiastically embracing Regi's model because it is clearly a more effective means of equipping next generation leaders than some of the programs we've tried in the past.

I'm sure you've seen a dozen or more curricula designed to help individuals become better at a variety of things. *Mentor Like Jesus* is not a curriculum. It's not a program. I'm tempted to call it the beginning of a movement. However, Regi would be quick to point out that it is actually an extension of a movement—a movement launched two thousand years ago when Jesus chose twelve men, poured His life into them, then sent them out to do the same.

I've had the opportunity to watch *Mentor Like Jesus* take shape over time. What began as an idea has now evolved into a well-thought-through, transferable, multiplication strategy. I've seen the results firsthand. Several of Regi's alumni work or volunteer on our campuses. Their lives are testimonies to the effectiveness of this approach to mentoring and to the principles Regi has poured into these young leaders.

I've been leaning on Regi Campbell's advice and counsel for ten years. I often find myself asking, "What would Regi do?" With the publication of *Mentor Like Jesus*, you too have the opportunity to lean into the wisdom and insights of a guy whose faith is big and whose commitment to personal ministry is absolutely contagious.

Well done, Regi.

—Andy Stanley

PREFACE

I love mentoring.

Next to my family, nothing else I've done has given me more satisfaction or fulfillment. Nothing.

Not making money. Not getting awards. Not traveling.

Nothing.

I can't really explain how I discovered it. There I was, teaching a singles Sunday school class at a large Baptist church outside Atlanta, Georgia. Although I had been a confessing Christian since childhood, I had been a genuine Christ follower for only a few years. But I was serious about making disciples, and I put a lot into this class, trying to inspire these young people to move God from a category to an intimate personal relationship. The class was growing, and I could see people "get it" . . . surrendering their lives to Jesus Christ and growing in their relationship with Him.

Each week it seemed one of the single guys would come up at the end of class or call me on Monday. "Hey, Regi, can we get together this week? I want to talk to you about my job" or "my girlfriend" or "my dad." I didn't think much of it. I was older than they were, fairly successful, and somewhat wise about the world.

A few days later we'd meet early in the morning at some breakfast place and dive into the issue the young man was facing. I would ask a lot of questions, leading him to think things through, and usually bringing him face-to-face with the wisdom of what God has to say in Scripture. Coffee finished, advice dispensed, and I was off to the office and to my "paying job."

Several hundred times this scenario was repeated over the course of thirteen years—until I heard a speaker say something that rocked my mentoring world. He said,

> **More time spent with fewer people equals greater kingdom impact.**

It suddenly dawned on me that I wasn't making the best use of my time . . . that I could make a greater impact for God by being more focused. Maybe I should pick a few of these bright young men and make a more serious commitment of time and energy to them. Instead of being issue-driven and reactive, I could be principle-driven and proactive, working into their lives the truth that God has shown me through my experience (i.e., mistakes) and what I've learned about life by applying His Word.

So I looked around my life—work world, church world, neighborhood and friends world—and picked out every young, married, high-potential guy that I knew. I targeted thirty-somethings because that was my age when I most needed a mentor but didn't have one. I sent these young men an e-mail and offered to spend a year (three hours a month) with them with the intention of teaching them what I've learned about God, marriage, business, fatherhood, and relationships. Twelve of the twenty-seven guys that I e-mailed replied and said they'd be interested, and I picked the eight that I thought I could help the most.

I called it "radical mentoring" because it seemed radical at the time. I now call it "next-generation mentoring," because it's really not radical . . . it's not even new. But more on that in a minute.

I believe this mentoring has had a significant impact. Lives have been changed, marriages have been saved, children have been dealt with in a more loving way, and my life has been incredibly blessed in the process.

But there's another major turn in the story of how this book came to be.

Not too long ago I awoke in the middle of the night with this thought:

This is what Jesus did!

It came to me that next-generation mentoring is a model that Jesus invented two thousand years ago. Unknowingly, I had stumbled onto a set of practices that should be obvious to all of us but until now haven't been.

We have visualized Jesus as CEO, Jesus as an environmentalist, and even thought about what Jesus' politics might have been. But in reality . . . in history . . . regardless of your religious beliefs, Jesus was a mentor. Those he mentored became totally committed to his mission, worked together as an effective team, and through their efforts, arguably one-third of the world's population believes in what they taught. From eleven people to two billion people . . . Jesus was a pretty good mentor.

Now I see that what I was doing wasn't really so radical after all. I was simply doing what Jesus did . . . investing in the next generation.

No wonder these mentoring groups have born such fruit. No wonder they've been so fulfilling for me. No wonder the guys who've gone through the mentoring year with me have seen their lives changed forever. And no wonder mentoring has become such a fulfilling and gratifying endeavor for me personally. I'm just following in the footsteps of the world's greatest mentor. I'm just doing what Jesus did with His disciples.

Wow.

Intentionally mentoring younger people in a group setting has been one of the most fulfilling things I've ever done. And those people whom I have inspired to follow this model and do the same thing have shared the same excitement. "I'll do this for the rest of my life," is a quote I hear.

In these pages I'll explain how next-generation mentoring works. I'll unpack a model for mentoring and show you how it's the model Jesus used with His disciples.

And if I'm successful, I'll inspire you to become a next-generation mentor. There's no age limit and no price for admission. Just a willingness to share. You'll find the best friends you've ever had, feel the most useful and fulfilled, and be blessed in ways that only the Father can bless you.

Come.

Read on.

INTRODUCTION

When you write a book, you're supposed to start off with some engaging story . . . some hook that will grab readers and keep them reading. That's the pressure point. I know that if I don't get your interest and attention right now, I'll have wasted all the time and effort in writing this book. And worse, you'll have missed the opportunity of a lifetime, not to mention the money you spent and the trees we'll have killed in the process.

To make it even more intense, I know I have one of the greatest secrets in the world to unveil. I know something that I've learned through my experience these last eight years that can change your life forever. I've discovered something that can be the answer to some of the questions baby boomers and half-timers are asking.

Believe me, millions of people are looking for answers to these questions; questions like:

- What should I do with the rest of my life?
- I want to make a difference, but how?

- Is going into vocational ministry the only way to please God?
- How can my life count for something?
- How do I connect with God and with others like me?
- How do I leave a legacy?
- How will future generations even know that I was here?

I've had those questions for years. I've read book after book, been to a ton of retreats and seminars, and had hundreds of discussions with other Christians.

As is often the case, the answer came in a way I didn't expect. The answer came from within the context of my own life and experience. And it came from the life of Jesus.

It's called mentoring.

Intentionally investing in the next generation . . . for God's glory.

I call it *next-generation mentoring.*

I have discovered a process, a model for mentoring that has given my life meaning and has had a profound effect on the folks I've invested in. It's not hard to do. It's natural and not burdensome. And it's life changing.

Here's what's really cool. I thought that I had made it up, but in reality Jesus did.

Next-generation mentoring is just doing what Jesus did.

For just a minute let's think about Jesus from a totally human perspective.

Jesus is one of the most admired figures in all of human history. A majority of Americans admire Jesus, whether they believe that He was God's Son or not.

Almost no one will say anything bad about Jesus. Jews, Muslims, Hindus, Buddhists. Everyone thinks well of Jesus.

Why? Jesus didn't bring any revolutionary teaching to the world. He was Jewish. He stood by and amplified Jewish law. He didn't create some new higher consciousness or begin a sociopolitical movement. He lived a somewhat normal life as a child and then became a significant historical and religious figure in the last three years of His life.

Jesus is so admired that writers have hypothesized what He would have been like in all kinds of roles. Charles Sheldon wrote the classic *In His Steps* in 1896. It has sold more than thirty million copies and is still in print. In it you're led to envision what Jesus would do if He faced the "day in the life" situations we face today.

A few years ago Laurie Beth Jones hypothesized what Jesus would have done as CEO. Others have offered their version of what Jesus would have been like as a voter, a politician, a teacher, an artist, a pastor, a leader, a husband, and a friend—all good stuff but more or less hypothetical.

What Jesus did that's inarguable is mentor! Jesus mentored twelve guys for three years. It's well documented . . . by four different authors, two of which were eyewitnesses *and* products of His mentoring process.

If there's anything we should be able to learn from Jesus and replicate in our own lives, it's mentoring. We have a documented model with proven results.

That's why I'm writing this book, to share with you what I've learned about mentoring the way Jesus did it.

What makes me an expert on this topic? Nothing. I'm not a theologian; I'm a businessman. And there's more that I don't know about mentoring than I do know. But almost by accident, and out of self-defense, I began intentionally mentoring younger guys about twenty years ago. Let me explain.

An Accidental Tourist

It was 1983. A relatively young but zealous Christians, my wife and I saw a need in our new church, and we volunteered to fill it . . . to work with single adults. There was no singles ministry . . . no singles Sunday school class . . . no singles anything. So we borrowed a living room from someone who lived near the church and started a singles group. It grew rapidly, and before long we had seventy single people connected to our lives and our family.

If you're over forty and want to give out advice, just let the twenty-something single guys in your church know that you're available. They'll be all over you, looking for input on everything from finding the right job to finding the right mate, finding the right church, finding the right color socks. You name it.

And thus it was. I got calls all the time, and I poured myself into helping these bright, energetic single people (I worked with the guys, for obvious reasons) with whatever happened to be their IOD (issue of the day).

One thing for sure . . . I was busy. I was also exhausted. I was meeting with guys all over Atlanta . . . breakfast, lunch, and dinner. I was serving up advice like Starbucks serves up lattes. I didn't know any better; I was serving the Lord by serving these folks, and God honored that with some spiritual breakthroughs for people here and there. But mostly I was just busy . . . spreading myself hopelessly thin trying to be all things to all God's (single) people.

Then I heard a speaker (author Tim Elmore who has since become a good friend) make this statement:

> **More time with fewer people equals greater kingdom impact.**

Wow.

You mean I don't have to spread my energy and influence to every single person who wants to buy me a cup of coffee?

You mean God might actually be more honored by my spending time with fewer people?

That didn't even seem American. Less rather than more?

I started exploring this new idea.

Fewer people . . . more time . . . greater kingdom impact.

A small group . . . that's it. I'll put together a small group of guys, spend focused time with them, and that will have greater kingdom impact than my current helter-skelter approach. Before you laugh, remember this was in 1983, before small groups became the buzz and the bomb they are today.

Some of the guys that I had invested so much in had begun to call me their mentor, so it was a natural for me to begin referring to them as my "mentoring group." Being raised Baptist and knowing that any group of people meeting together had to have a curriculum, I set out to find one for my not-yet-formed mentoring group.

This is where it gets interesting.

Every curriculum I saw looked like Sunday school (no disrespect intended!). I wanted to share my life with these guys . . . teach them from my own experience . . . share plays from my own playbook, to use a football analogy. But every guide I looked at seemed canned, stiff, and programmed.

Those are words that no one ever used to describe me as a person, so how could I possibly be passionate about doing it that way? Is this going to be another Sunday school class where everyone sits in rows, looks up answers, fills in blanks, and walks away unaffected?

So I made a decision.

I'll make up a process. It'll be uniquely mine. I'll share what I've learned about the Bible, about God, about business, about family . . . about life. I'll pick some young guys that I see potential in, invite them to join in, and we'll see what happens.

And that's how *next-generation mentoring* got started.

Little did I know that the process I made up harmonizes amazingly with how Jesus mentored His disciples.

I have tweaked the process a little each year, making some small changes and smoothing out the rough edges. But in the main the next-generation mentoring process that I will tell you about in the pages that follow is the same as it was when I discovered it in 2000. I've seen awesome results (I guess most Christians call it "fruit") and have helped several other men become next-generation mentors. Only recently did I discover the similarities between the process that I came up with and the process Jesus used.

These are the key ingredients of next-generation mentoring. You'll quickly see that they are exactly the same as those that Jesus used.

1. It's **on purpose**. It's all about the Father and kingdom building. Jesus was on a mission, and mentoring was the key strategy to fulfill His mission.
2. It's a **selfless** endeavor. Jesus mentored out of obedience to the Father. He got nothing out of it personally. He simply responded to God's call on His life and did what the Father led Him to do.
3. It starts in a **group** context, not one-on-one. Jesus knew the value of interaction of group members with one another.

The group became a community, inextractable from one another. Jesus also accepted and even promoted the "group within the group" that invariably develops. He had favorites, and He didn't hide it or apologize for it. Yes, there was powerful one-on-one interaction, but it started in the context of the group.

4. Jesus **handpicked** those He mentored after prayer. The group was made up of laypeople, not "church people" . . . diverse . . . anything but a holy huddle. The mentor-mentoree relationship was acknowledged. It was not a peer-to-peer group; it was a mentor-mentoree construct . . . clear and unapologetic.

5. It was for a short, **defined period of time.** Jesus' mentoring program began on time and ended on time. There was a graduation day when His mentorees were commissioned and launched.

6. At the core of Jesus' teaching was **Scripture.** Jesus and His mentorees knew the Scriptures by heart. The Word guided their decision making. Jesus helped His guys understand and apply God's Word.

7. Public and private **prayer** was huge, public, and private. Jesus modeled a prayerful life; He taught the disciples how to pray and prayed with them and for them.

8. Jesus **modeled** His faith in a transparent way. Jesus lived out His life in front of His mentorees. They became like family to Him. They saw how He applied His faith, how He struggled, how He handled stress, and how He handled dying.

9. Jesus **taught along the way** of life. He was practical yet spiritual. Jesus helped His guys with practical situations . . . everything from taxes to workplace issues, from goal setting to family relations. He was far more practical than hypothetical. They discussed the law for sure, but Jesus taught from His knowledge and experience.

10. There was a **mutual commitment,** and it was a huge commitment. They left their businesses, families, homes . . . all to follow and learn. Jesus never gave up on them,

even when they failed and ran away. Ultimately they never gave up on Jesus, giving their lives not for His memory or His teachings but for His kingdom.

11. It had a **required multiplication** element. It produced evangelists and disciple makers. Multiplication was a part of what every one signed up for, and no one was excluded from that requirement.

Together, the elements yielded a group of committed Christ followers. Those guys got it. They created their own groups of mentorees, and those mentorees created more groups. (Somewhere along the line they started being called churches.) What resulted is the greatest movement of all time. From this first mentoring group, billions of people became followers of Jesus Christ. The institution of the church was created. Health care, education, and social service institutions that carry the name of Christ all trace their origins back to this first mentoring group led by Jesus.

In these pages we'll take each of these eleven practices and explore what Jesus did and how we can emulate Him today. Having led groups using this approach for the last eight years, I'll bring the principles alive with stories and examples of what to do and what not to do.

If you're holding this book in your hand or reading this excerpt online, and you're interested in the idea of mentoring, then you're probably in one of four camps.

Camp 1. You appreciate mentoring and would like to do it, if only you knew how. You understand the value of being mentored. You may have even had a mentor yourself . . . but declaring yourself a mentor is beyond what you can see. And even if you could see it, you don't feel comfortable about the who, what, when, where, or how of mentoring a group of men or women. We're going to give you a plan and a track to run on.

Camp 2. You want a mentor but haven't been able to find one. You've seen other folks with these incredible mentors who have added so much to their lives. Yet you wonder: *How in the world does that happen? Where would I ever find a mentor like that?* We're going to share some practical steps you can take to find a mentor and engage him or her.

Camp 3. You've heard the term but never really given mentoring much thought. The idea of having a mentor is somewhat intriguing to you, but it's certainly not a felt need. And the idea of being a mentor to someone else is a totally new thought to you. Read on with an open mind. This *is* what Jesus did, and if you want to be a follower of Jesus, you have to go where He goes and do what He does. So hear me out and see where it leads.

Camp 4. You're someone who's just curious about Jesus . . . what He did, what He was like, how He interacted with people. This book will give you insight to Jesus as a mentor. You'll see Him in action as He taught, loved, challenged, forgave, and encouraged His guys. This is the first time (that I'm aware of) that Jesus has been looked at through the lens of a modern-day mentor.

The overarching motivation of this book is to inspire you to become a next-generation mentor.

"But why? Why should I do this?"

I'll give you six reasons to be a next-generation mentor.

Reason 1. Jesus did it, and He told you to as well. We have visualized Jesus as CEO, Jesus as environmentalist, and even thought about what Jesus' politics might have been. But in reality . . . in history . . . regardless of your religious beliefs, *Jesus was a mentor.* His mentorees became totally committed to His mission, worked together as an effective team, and through their efforts, arguably one-third of the world's population believes in what they taught. From eleven people to two billion people . . . Jesus was a pretty good mentor.

And His final instruction to us before He returned to His place in heaven with the Father was what? "Go and make disciples" (Matt. 28:19). He's telling us, *"Go and do what I did. Go and find some people who are a little farther behind you on the path, and help them take their next steps, just as I did with my disciples!"* His call is universal. It transcends gender. It certainly transcends vocations since none of Jesus' mentorees were church people (nor was He).

Throughout this book we'll be looking at *how* He did what He did and achieved the success that He did. We'll look at the practices Jesus used to mentor His disciples. Is there a better place to look for best practices than to Jesus? And those practices are there . . . visible . . . right there in the Scriptures . . . for all to see and apply.

Reason 2. You'll find meaning and fulfillment. We spend hours, days, and years of our lives at work, often mindlessly plying our skills and experience in order to do good work and to get paid. We accumulate things, we experience places and events, we build picture albums of places we've been and the people we have shared them with. Yet within thirty seconds of our last breath, those memories will be gone, just like the unsaved document on our computer screen when the power goes out.

A friend was telling me about going through his parents' things after his dad (his last surviving parent) passed away. The pictures of places in the Holy Land, pictures from Italy and Greece, pictures from England and France . . . all thrown in a garbage bag and destroyed. Why? Because those pictures were only relevant to the person who took them, and when he or she passed on to the next part of their existence, the pictures became irrelevant and, thus, useless. Memories are that way; they are only meaningful to the person who experienced the thing that created them. And when the power is unplugged on that brain, they disappear.

In the opulence of Western culture, we spend the majority of our time and money making memories for ourselves and our loved ones. And as we do, we are drawn farther and farther away from having meaning in our lives.

Pursuing meaning in our lives doesn't exclude having great memories, but meaning matters in a deeper and a more long-lasting way. Meaning says that the activity that you're involved with is really important. Meaning says that it matters at a deep level. Meaning says the consequences of the activity will affect the people involved for a long time. Meaning says that there is a multiplier effect, that future generations of people will benefit from the thing that has meaning.

Mentoring a group of younger people gives life meaning. To know that you have shown them something that will help them avoid some major mistake, which means they and those closest to them may avoid the painful consequences of that mistake . . . that is fulfilling. To watch a younger person choose to become a volunteer leader with Young Life instead of becoming the weekly trivia champion at the local sports bar . . . that is meaning. To watch one of your mentorees become an influential leader in his church . . . that is meaning. To watch a protégé lead his family through an incredible family crisis in a godly way . . . that is meaning.

Reason 3. It'll sharpen you and keep you sharp. Intentionally mentoring a group of younger people is also a great opportunity for the mentor to learn and to refresh knowledge that he already has. As the saying goes, "We teach what we most need to learn." As you go through the process of reviewing what you've learned, you will rediscover things you have overlooked or forgotten . . . skills that are so much a part of your unconscious competence yet have been sitting on the shelf for years. What about that seminar you attended on listening skills? When you dust off the content and start picking the best parts to share with your group, you find yourself again practicing better listening skills. As you share the principles you've learned with your mentorees, you learn them all over again yourself.

You will also find that these younger people have some things that they know and can share with you and the group as well . . . it's a symbiotic process that breathes new life into the mentor as you share what you know and get your knowledge base expanded at the same time.

Reason 4. It'll make you more grateful. Mentoring a small group of younger people will only be successful if it's done from the overflow of gratitude from a grateful heart. Many Christians will hear a sermon or read a book and be motivated by the desire to "be good" or do something good. Others may feel guilty for their past lives, saying, "You know, I owe God so much, I want to pay Him back." Still others may be motivated by pride. It is kind of a rush to have a group of people say they want to hang out with you for a year just to learn from you.

The only consistent, long-term motivation for the Christian to be selfless and to serve others is gratitude for what God has done for them. This deep sense of gratitude stems from one of three sources. Most of the time you'll find "givers" (mentors will almost always be givers) have experienced significant life change. They were serious sinners, and Christ led them to a 180 . . . a complete turnaround in their lives. These folks know what their lives were like without Him, and they have now experienced a different kind of life, one that stands for something and is pretty much free of intentional sin. A deep sense of gratitude stems from the rescue of their lives.

A second group of givers base their gratitude on some event or crisis in their life, where God intervened and saved them or their loved ones from a catastrophe. Their motivation is pure . . . not trying to pay God back; they are just deeply grateful for His mercy. Often they sense that God preserved them for a reason. That sense of being alive for some kingdom purpose provides a lasting source of motivation, and becoming a next-generation mentor *may be* a part of why they were protected and preserved to live another season.

A third group of highly motivated givers haven't had any significant near-death experiences, nor have they been rescued from a life of deep, dark sin. They just seem to grasp the significance of the cross and the love that God has for them. Responding to God's loving call on their lives, they love, they serve, they give . . . they just seem to get it somehow. These people make great mentors because they've known God for a long time. They are "steady Eddie" faithful followers; and they can tell a confident, long-term, life story to their mentorees. These days we often overlook the testimonies of the good guys who have been faithful from a young age. We think it's more compelling to highlight the cataclysmic repentance of the former drug addict, adulterer, or drunk because that more dramatically displays the power of God. God's power is just as powerfully displayed when people are raised in Christian homes, protected from all that waywardness, quietly come to the Father as new believers, and take their place in their families and churches. Think about how rare that is these days. Don't you think God has a plan to leverage that experience? Wouldn't you like to have your son mentored by someone like that?

As I became an intentional mentor through my next-generation mentoring groups, I became a more grateful person. I was able to thank God for allowing me to make those painful mistakes because now others could benefit from those mistakes as well as myself. I paid the price for my stupidity. How grateful I am when God uses that price, my mistakes, as life lessons for younger guys, giving them the chance to avoid the same mistakes. Who would have ever thought I'd be grateful for my screwups?

The other day as I was praying, I heard myself say, "Lord, thank you so much for giving me such a great life. I'm eternally grateful that the sins of my youth have been forgiven and that you've used the pain and learning from them to encourage and equip my younger brothers. Thank you for using me to help them avoid those mistakes and their corresponding consequences."

Reason 5. You'll leave a real, living legacy. Not too long ago I read where a business school was offering to be named after any donor who would give a million and a half dollars. Another school took on the name of a rich donor, only to have to withdraw the name after the rich donor became no longer rich.

When some people in their nineties were surveyed several years ago, they were asked this question: "What are the three things you wish you had done that you didn't do?"

The answers were somewhat surprising but not really.

"Take more risk." That one was a bit of a surprise.

"Reflect more." Again, somewhat unexpected.

"Focus more on things that will live beyond me."

Legacy. We all want to leave a legacy.

The word *legacy* gets a lot of play these days. I believe that's because baby boomers, those born between 1946 and 1964, are beginning to slow down, retire, and reflect. They're asking questions like, "How have I spent my life?" and, "Ten years from now, how will anyone know that I was even here?"

That's why having a building named for you sort of scratches the itch. It says, "I was somebody. I did something that mattered."

I'll compare my legacy with anyone (excluding Billy Graham and Bill Bright of course). Here's why:

In the past eight years, I've intentionally mentored sixty-four guys. Most report that they have a deeper, more meaningful walk with Jesus than they did before the next-generation mentoring experience. They are disciples . . . learners and followers of Jesus. To my knowledge none have fallen away. All are still married. All are involved in a church. All are attempting to raise their kids in the faith. And from what I can tell, they are, to varying degrees, walking with God.

All of these mentorees have signed a covenant saying they'll mentor at least one group of eight after they're forty (when they know something). Most will mentor many groups, but let's just assume that they do the minimum. And let's assume that their mentorees sign a similar covenant and mentor eight guys before they die.

If that process continues for just five generations there will be more than one million Christ followers that God somehow allowed me to be used in their lives. Unbelievable, huh?

I wanted to call this book *How to Have a Big Funeral*, because if just 10 percent of these mentorees showed up at my funeral, it'd be one of the biggest in history. But then I read what Louis Grizzard, an author and a longtime columnist for the *Atlanta Journal Constitution* said: "The primary determinant of the size of a man's funeral is the weather that day." So I let that idea go.

But seriously, God has blessed me with an incredible legacy.

And the exact same legacy is waiting for you. All you have to do is become a next-generation mentor and let God start using you to help younger Christ followers take their next step, share with them "a piece of your map" . . . let God use you as "iron" to "sharpen iron" (Prov. 27:17).

In the pages that follow, I'm going to show you how. And the really cool thing is that I'm just going to show you what Jesus did. It's that simple.

Reason 6. You won't waste your life. I have had several moments of truth in my life, but one of the most important happened when I heard a speaker ask this question:

"If your life were a dollar, how are you spending it?"

That question creates laser focus.

- What am I doing with my life?
- Am I more than just another "piece of the machine"?
- Did God put me here just to go to church and then die and go to heaven?

John Piper, in his book *Don't Waste Your Life*, gives this perspective:

> I will tell you what a tragedy is. I will show you how to waste your life. Consider a story in the February 1998 edition of the *Readers Digest*, which tells about a couple who "took early retirement from their jobs in the Northeast when he was 59 and she was 51. Now they live in Punta Gorda, Florida, where they cruise on their 30 foot trawler, play softball, and collect shells." At first, when I read it I thought it might be a joke. A spoof on the American dream. But it

wasn't. Tragically, this was the dream: Come to the end of your life—your one and only precious, God-given life—and let the last great work of your life, before you give an account to your Creator, be this: playing softball and collecting shells. Picture them before Christ at the great day of judgment. "Look, Lord. See my shells." That is a tragedy. And people are spending billions of dollars to persuade you to embrace that tragic dream. Over against that, I put my protest: Don't buy it. Don't waste your life.[1]

As we pass forty, as our kids grow up and need us less and less, and as we progress in our careers and financial success, it's incredibly tempting just to enjoy life. The place at the lake beckons, the vacations get longer and more exotic, and the focus on our lives becomes increasingly selfish. That's why so many voices in the Christian community are talking about "finishing well," about resisting the temptation to withdraw from engagement with others and staying in the game.

I don't think God is going to care only about how you served Him when you were young. My Bible doesn't say, "Make disciples until you get a few bucks" or "until you retire and move to the mountains." It says to make disciples, and I believe that at least part of the reason God gives some people more money, free time, and wisdom is so they can invest in those who are coming after them. I can see God smile over that investment much more than I can see Him smiling over a +4 golf handicap.

Don't waste your life. Do what Jesus did. Pick some less experienced people and mentor them. I'll show you how.

---1---

MENTORING ON
PURPOSE

In his book *Apple Confidential*, Owen W. Linzmayer tells of the interaction between John Scully and Steve Jobs, the founder and chief of Apple Computer. Scully, then the legendary CEO of Pepsico, tells how he repeatedly turned down Jobs's compelling offers to come head up Apple. Until one day when Jobs said something that rocked Scully's world,

> "Do you want to spend the rest of your life selling sugared water, or do you want a chance to change the world?"[2]

That was the defining moment. Scully changed his mind, quit one of the most lucrative, high-profile CEO positions in America, and moved to California to join the team of this small, upstart computer company with a vision.

Here's the question I'm putting to you,

> "Do you want to change the world?"

Jesus did.

Jesus told us His purpose. Recorded by His best friend on Earth, John, He said, "I have come that they might have life, and have it to the full" (John 10:10).

What did He mean by "life" and by "have it to the full"?

Jesus gave us life by rescuing us from death. Yes, that sounds vague and metaphoric, but it's not. It's real and matter of fact. We would have died, and that would have been it. Game over. We would have had no hope beyond the grave.

But because Jesus fulfilled His life purpose, we know that men will die and still live. Jesus did. He died a public, undeniable death and then miraculously and supernaturally came back to life, showing Himself to His mentorees and to five hundred other people. If He did that, I'm in for whatever He says I need to do that can allow me to do that too. That's not all He meant by giving us "life," but it's a huge part of it.

But more, He wanted to show us the kind of life that God intended for us to have. A life filled with meaning and wonder . . . as close to the life that Adam and Eve had before they declared their independence and decided that they knew better than God how to have the best life now.

That life, that "God life," is a life of purpose.

Purpose-led Living

I recently heard a speaker addressing the question of longevity. He said everyone needs to get up every day with something to do—some duty, task, calling, some purpose—a reason to be.

When I think about the life Jesus lived, the life He modeled for me, I see someone who loved and served people. He was intentional about it. And when I try to understand that last part of His purpose statement . . . "and have it to the full" . . . I think I understand what He meant.

As Christians, when we accept the Father's offer of salvation through Jesus, we get "life" . . . eternal life. And we get a life of peace while we finish out our days here on Earth.

But if we want the second part, "and have it (life) to the full," we have to move beyond the gift of our salvation. We have to want more.

We have to get involved in the cause that Jesus started . . . the cause of redemption. We have to become others focused. We have to start thinking outside our own little world and ask God: "How can I help? What would You have me do? I know that my purpose is to bring glory to You . . . to make You more famous, but how would You have me do that? Help me find my unique purpose in Your kingdom!"

The *p* word is certainly everywhere today. Since Rick Warren wrote *The Purpose Driven Life* and sold a gazillion copies, everyone wants to talk about purpose. That's because it's important, and when we talk about something as vague as mentoring, then purpose becomes even more important. But let's get clear on the terminology.

A mission or goal is about *what*. It's measurable and finite. If my mission is to become a CPA, then I know *what* I have to do, and I'll know *when* I complete the mission.

Strategies and tactics are about *how*. When we strategize, we think about how we use our time, talent, and treasure to accomplish the mission or achieve our goal. My strategy to become a CPA might include doing an internship, going back to college, working for an accounting firm for a year, studying my brains out at night, and then sitting for the CPA exam five years from now. That's a strategy to accomplish a goal or mission.

But purpose is about *why*. It's not really measurable. It's understandable yet vague. Warren's mantra is that we're all created for a specific purpose . . . to glorify God. And he's right. That is the overarching purpose of every person and every thing. God created everything for His glory. We are His highest and greatest creation, created in His image.

He created us because He wanted a family, and He sent Jesus to become His "adoption agency" for us. The paperwork is all filled out . . . the fees are paid. All we have to do to complete the adoption process is to believe.

Once we're adopted, we're irrevocably in His family. We can't be "unadopted," just as an adopted child in America can't be unadopted. It's a status that isn't changed because of bad behavior or anything else. It's permanent.

Now that we are God's children, what do we do with our lives that will make our Father in heaven proud of us . . . make Him glad that He adopted us?

Become like Him. Become like our loving, kind, wise, disciplined Father. To make Himself understandable to us, our God became one of us and lived on the earth for a while, in view of a bunch of eyewitnesses (a few of which He inspired to write down what they heard and saw), and modeled what He wanted us *to be* like.

Mentoring is not about coming *to know* something; that would be education. Mentoring isn't about learning *to do* something; that would be training.

Mentoring is about showing someone how *to be something.* It's about *becoming* a learner and follower of Jesus Christ because that's what makes our Father most pleased. It's also what makes Jesus most famous because millions of us are running around the world emulating Jesus. And as someone said, you only know that you're a follower of Jesus when you've helped someone else become a follower of Jesus. That's what next-generation mentoring can do, and with enough men and women becoming active followers of Jesus, we can change the world.

About 350 years after Christ, the Roman emperor Julian (AD 332–363) wanted to reinstitute faithfulness to the pagan religions of Rome but struggled because Christians were doing such good things for people, even strangers, that they rendered the Roman gods irrelevant.

Wouldn't it be cool to render the pagan gods of the twenty-first century irrelevant by having millions of Christ followers become so genuine in their faith that they changed the world with their kindness, mercy, and generosity?

I believe that can happen. Not through televangelism, crusades, or megachurches . . . but through mentoring. We must emulate what Jesus did—help men and women become learners and followers of Jesus Christ with a passion and commitment to pay it forward to others.

Mentoring Is Messy

Modern-day church people love classes, seminars, Bible studies, and small groups. We show up, sit in circles or rows, listen, share, pray, eat, and leave. Usually we do some homework in between meetings, but it's not too much (by design because we don't want to have fewer people involved by making it too hard . . . more on that later).

It's neat. It's predictable. It's noninvasive. It's easily merged into our wrinkle-free lives.

Mentoring is different. There isn't a curriculum per se. There isn't a video with discussion questions. There isn't a form you fill out at the end that says, "Joe Smith has completed blankety-blank course."

You can get dirty mentoring people. They bring real issues to the table. And those issues require mentors to get personal, transparent, and exposed. One of the most common phrases a mentor says is, "I don't know. I can tell you what I did when . . . Here's how it turned out. Here's what I wish I had done. Here's what Jesus said about it. Here's what I missed."

Many times I've left meetings with mentorees and gone to my knees asking God, "Why is this happening to him? I don't get it." Many times I've prayed for one of my mentorees' situations, and not only did I not get my prayer answered, but I sensed God was totally silent.

Then I realized my role . . . to help the younger ones interpret what's happening the right way, the scriptural way . . . the God way. Through it all, I'm practicing my own faith and making it stronger.

My Purpose

Other than my intimate relationship with the Father, nothing has given me more direction in life than my life purpose statement. Without it I probably wouldn't be a mentor.

Earlier I mentioned *The Purpose Driven Life* and Rick Warren's assertion that we are all here to "glorify God." I agree.

But how? How do we glorify God? How can we make our lives be a praise to Him?

After a lot of thinking, praying, and editing, my life purpose statement was finally settled:

> "I, Regi Campbell, glorify God by loving and serving
> others and by challenging them to be all they can be
> and to give all of themselves to Jesus Christ."

Do you see the three operative words—*love, serve,* and *challenge?* Let me explain.

Love. It's inarguable that Christ followers are to love God and love one another. *Love* is a verb, not only a noun. Love that is real is demonstrated. When Jesus told us that the greatest commandment is to "love the Lord your God with all your heart, soul, mind, and strength, and to love your neighbor as yourself," He meant to do it and not just talk about it.

The second word is *serve*. This is where love takes action. Rick Warren, in a recent talk to the Catalyst Conference, said, "The church has amputated its hands and its feet, and all that's left is its mouth." We talk about serving, but in large part we serve the institution of the church. We serve each other within the church . . . and that's about it.

Mentoring younger ones puts hands and feet onto loving and serving. That's why everyone who has maturity in the faith can do it. And everyone who needs maturity in the faith needs to be mentored.

The third word is where it gets dicey. My third word is *challenge*. I'm a challenger. When I wrote down my philosophy of life when it comes to relationships, it's "to bring a smile to the face and reflection to the heart of every person I meet."

I heard a sermon yesterday at a church in another city. The well-meaning pastor said, "You are each created for a specific purpose . . . specific only to you. It's up to you to go out there and discover what that purpose is and fulfill it."

As my friend John says, "That's like telling me to go stand in the corner of a round room!"

How on Earth are we to figure out what our unique purpose is? Just to think about it is daunting. We're all so different. How could we each have a unique purpose? Yet I believe it's out there . . . that God wired, gifted, and experienced each of us differently; for His unique purpose and calling to His kingdom work.

When I engage with my mentorees, there's a strong sense of challenge in the air. I start by challenging them to be on time, somewhat of a lost practice in our culture and particularly in church world. I challenge them by requiring them to do their homework assignments. I challenge them to be open and transparent. I'll ask personal questions and demand honest answers. I test their assumptions. I question the premise of their assumptions. I force them to consider what God says about the situation in His Word. Because that's how I'm wired. That's the purpose God built into me. He will use me and that challenging gift in the lives of my mentorees, but only for a defined period of time.

I won't be the last or only mentor these guys will have. I'm in their lives for one year. God may bring an encourager into their lives after their year with me. Or a coach sometime after that. I'm only responsible for being what I am, doing what the Lord wired me to do, and using the gifts, talents, and experiences that He's placed in me.

Since Jesus was the only complete mentor, the only mentor who could fully challenge and encourage, then I can't possibly be all of these things for my mentorees. My prayer is that they will learn all they can from me but then move on to be mentored by others in the future. In my dreams churches would form teams of mentors, understand their particular gifts and purposes, and connect mentorees with mentors sequentially so that people would be intentionally exposed to multiple mentors and their various offerings.

Outcomes

What does next-generation mentoring look like when it's done? What are we shooting for here?

For me, it's about producing more godly men.

Vague? Yes. But it is what it is.

But what a BHAG . . . big, hairy, audacious goal!

I want every guy that goes through the mentoring year with me to become a more godly man and a more serious Christ follower.

And to be more specific:

- I want these men to know God personally . . . to have a clear picture of God. Who He is. How God looks at them as adopted sons. And how they view God as the perfect Father who loves them immeasurably.
- I want them to embrace Scripture in a new and different way. They will commit specific verses to memory by topic so they can call the verses up and apply them to real-world situations. In addition, I want them to appreciate the entire Bible and to see how it provides answers to the questions of life.
- I want them to understand spiritual warfare—what it is, how it is played out in the twenty-first century, and how prayer can affect what's going on in the invisible realm.

- I want them to love the church and commit to it, as it is unquestionably God's chosen vehicle for this and all future generations.
- I want them to have God's perspective on money and possessions.
- I want them to know how to make good decisions, building those decisions on wisdom and on good theology.
- I want them to understand God's perspective on marriage and how to live out their role.
- I want them to trust God in every aspect of their lives . . . to pray, seek counsel, make wise decisions, and *move forward*, trusting God for all the outcomes.
- I want them to fulfill and enjoy their roles as godly fathers.
- I want them to accept their responsibility to be intentional about influencing the people in their sphere of influence to move one step closer to Christ . . . to be intentional disciple makers.

That's a tall order, especially for a regular guy like me who has business, family, church, and other ministry things to do. And all this should happen in one year?

Obviously, God has to do something special if progress on these goals is to happen in that short a time frame. And so He's intimately involved in the process: loving, challenging, affirming, stretching—all the things a perfect father would do as He raises a son.

It's also cool that the mentorees are getting help from the "best and brightest" of our generation. As they read, they're mentored by the authors—Andy Stanley, Gordon MacDonald, Gary Smalley, and others. A lot can happen in a year when you sit at the feet of teachers like these.

Inside Out

Next-generation mentoring works because it starts with the inner man and his relationship with his heavenly Father. With clarity in that relationship, focus moves to the way the inner man thinks, acts, and then relates first with himself and then with his wife, children, and the rest of his relationships in the world.

Jesus' purpose translated into action.

Jesus' choice of mentoring a small group of followers to effect His mission was a brilliant decision. Just do the math: twelve disciples, multiplying themselves over and over, and the number of people getting the message is overwhelming. There was no more effective way to get an important message out in the first century with no Internet, TV, or direct mail. What's really cool is that today, even with all that technology, individual influence, word of mouth, multiplication is still the most powerful way to communicate a message. Companies spend billions today to create brands, viral marketing, and buzz, all for the purpose of spreading the message quickly and effectively to millions of people.

And the message that Jesus has is unique. It's not about a theology or a doctrine as much as it is about a man . . . His origin, His life, His death, His resurrection, and His purpose for the world. In the first-century world there was no more powerful communications vehicle than the firsthand account of an eyewitness who saw something. That was the first step in God's plan to reveal the message of Jesus: to have Him "live out loud" in front of a small group of people, His disciples, and thus position them to describe firsthand what they heard and saw.

The Mentoree Perspective from Richard Chancy

I'm Richard Chancy, and as Regi takes you through mentoring as Jesus did it, I'll chime in with how it looks from my perspective . . . that of a mentoree. I was in Regi's seventh group, but I've gotten feedback from most of the guys who were in all of the other groups. I'll try to speak for them as well.

I'm a relentless self-help junkie. When I graduated from college, the first book I read cover to cover was *The Power of Positive Thinking* by Norman Vincent Peale. It was the first book I had ever voluntarily read. After that I was hooked on self-improvement. I read anything I can get my hands on that has to do with professional, spiritual, or physical growth.

When I had the opportunity to be mentored on a personal level by Regi Campbell, I was all in. In my circle, Regi is known as "a rock-star" Christian business guy, and this mentoring group was a pretty hot ticket. I had to go through a selection process which, by the way, I didn't make it through the first time I tried. But once I was in, I was all the way in, and I brought some specific expectations with me.

I hoped to get a few things in particular out of this group. I'm a networker, and I have a knack for building long-lasting relationships. Connecting with Regi and some other new guys was appealing. I had the opportunity to make friendships that will be lifelong.

Another expectation I had was to have a high level of accountability. I don't know how much of that is a result of my drive for personal growth or my competitive nature, but I desire to be held to a high standard. I felt that next-generation mentoring would be a pretty intense season as far as accountability was concerned.

The main reason I was interested, however, was Regi's business acumen. I have been fortunate to work in environments on every part of the spectrum from nonprofit ministries to for-profit companies owned by Christians, to one of the largest brokerages on Wall Street. But the one thing my career most lacked was true entrepreneurial guidance.

Regi had been a part of several tech start-ups, as well as being on the ground floor of helping my church, North Point Community Church, get started. Who better to learn from than a guy with all that experience? So I packed my expectations up and got started.

Why I'd Do It Again

I want to make sure that I draw a clear line for you between what I expected from mentoring and what I actually got out of it. There is a dramatic difference, and I was surprised by the growth I saw and continue to see. I had one plan, and God had another.

The biggest "aha" from my mentoring experience came from developing my purpose statement. We were asked to fill in these blanks:

"I exist to serve by _____ _____."

This statement had a deep effect on me for two reasons: (1) "I exist" assumes that we were created for a reason. (2) "To serve" means that my existence is about serving God and other people.

For several days I focused . . . thinking . . . praying . . . allowing God to guide me. Then I got the answer. God placed two words on my heart . . . *igniting passion*. I exist to serve by *igniting passion*. This statement was a revelation for me. I was both overwhelmed and humbled by what it could mean to ignite passion. I found my focus, and I'm living out of my strengths more than ever. Igniting passion is what I'm trying to do here. I want to ignite passion in you for mentoring!

It's hard to predict exactly what you'll experience or what you'll learn about yourself during the mentoring year. It will require more of you than you may be used to giving. But the way of Christ always does. God, in His infinite wisdom, knows that I'd have bailed on being mentored before it even began if I knew how tough it would be to learn the lessons that I learned. Now I'm confident that this season of being invested in, of being mentored, will yield a return for the rest of my life and then some.

Looking back, I don't think I ever stopped to think about why Regi would take the time to do this. Here is a guy that appears to be on top of the world. He's had tremendous success and is now just getting to the point of enjoying life and watching his children enjoy theirs. So in a world of "me first," why would he take the time to mentor a group of guys who think they have it all figured out?

The answer is simple.

Regi mentors because God led him to mentor. He simply obeyed.

I don't know what led you to pick up this book, but if you're reading this, maybe God is telling you to do the same thing.

Maybe now is a good time to do a half-time report. Look at your life and ask yourself, "How's it going?" Is it time to stop and evaluate . . . maybe take on a new challenge? If so, I hope you'll strongly consider walking the path with a group of guys for a year as a mentor. You won't regret it.

2

IT'S NOT ABOUT ME

"A society grows great when old men plant trees
whose shade they will never sit in."
—Greek Proverb

When I kick off my next-generation mentoring group each year, I surprise everyone with a pop test. Each mentoree has written a biographical summary of his history, and I've sent every mentoree copies of everyone's bio.

Problem is, they come to the first session and haven't read them. The scores are abysmal, sometimes in the low teens on a scale of one hundred. They're always highly embarrassed.

Why? Why do they not at least read about the guys they are going to be in a group with for a year?

Everyone is interested in his own deal . . . not anyone else's. I ask the convicting question, "If tonight you had been coming to a meeting of big potential customers who could help you make your sales quota or a group of senior corporate executives who could help you with your career, what would your score have been?" You bet they would spend the effort if they thought there was something in it for them. But just focusing on the other people in the group, learning about their families, careers, accomplishments for no apparent reason? Just to let them know that you're interested or that you care . . . why bother?

Authentic mentoring, mentoring like Jesus did, involves selflessness. It says, "I'm going to give to you . . . put you first . . . let you learn from my mistakes, and get nothing in return." In a sense the mentor says, "I've paid the price (via my mistakes) to learn what I've learned. I'm going to give you the benefit of that price so you won't have to pay it." Sounds a little like Jesus' deal for us, doesn't it?

Now that offer, that transaction, doesn't make sense in our economy. It's ludicrous. Why should you gain from my sacrifice? It's every man for himself, right?

But God's reality, the visible world merged with the invisible world, is a reality of threes, not twos.

Let me explain.

Deciding to mentor isn't a decision that's just between me and that person or me and that group. That's a world of twos.

It's me, the younger person who needs a mentor, and God. It's me, the potential next-generation mentoring group, and God.

God is the third party in every transaction . . . every situation . . . every decision.

Our relationship with God isn't as simple and straightforward as just being between Him and me or you. He's always using a third party—our wives, our kids, our pastor, our boss. He's always connecting us with people for His purposes. It's *always* "You and me, God." It's always, "Jesus, what would You have me do?" It's always three, not two.

As you consider the idea of becoming a next-generation mentor . . . to mentor like Jesus did, remember that there's a third party in the decision. He loves selflessness. He loves the servant heart. He loves for us to do what He did. He'll answer you if you'll consult Him about what He'd have you do.

Modeling Selflessness in the Twenty-first Century

In a society of self-reliance, how does one demonstrate genuine selflessness? Do you hold open the door for people entering the mall and never go in yourself? Do you give away all your money and possessions and become a monk?

Next-generation mentoring starts with selflessness on the part of the mentor. There has to be a drive or a calling to give back . . . to pay it forward. A commitment to the cause calls the mentor above selfish interest and toward selflessness.

Jesus was the only selfless human ever to walk the face of the earth. Think about it.

- He owned nothing so He could travel light and be totally focused on others.
- He gave up family to be about His mission.
- He often provided free food for people who were listening to His teaching.
- He helped fishermen catch fish.
- He healed people left and right and never asked for anything in return (not exactly the model for modern-day health care!). Often He asked people He healed not to tell anyone so that He didn't even get the credit publicly.

Jesus even gave up His family for His Father's business. We saw it when, at the age of twelve, He stayed behind in the synagogue to talk with the rabbis, causing His family great distress when they found that He was missing.

Then as an adult, He traveled throughout the country healing and preaching, often at risk to His life. Once when His family found Him, Jesus let them know in no uncertain terms that His ministry . . . the mentoring of His disciples . . . the teaching, healing, and miraculous casting out of demons . . . was more important than anything, even family (see Luke 8:18–21).

We know Jesus loved His family, so it wasn't that He abandoned them out of anger or rejection. One of His last acts from the cross was to ensure that John, His best friend, would care for His mom.

It's just that the "work of His Father" . . . that selfless work of revealing what God is really like and of mentoring His disciples to carry the work of His Father forward after His ascension, took a priority over things He might have selfishly enjoyed.

But the "biggie" is His death on the cross. Jesus voluntarily gave His life so that we could be forgiven for our sins and have eternal life.

What did Jesus get in return for this? Nothing. There was no quid pro quo. It was the ultimate act of selflessness . . . to give His life for the very people who were killing Him. That defines selflessness to me.

The selflessness of a good mentor is obvious. There's a willingness to invest time in others when there is no return on investment for yourself, at least nothing tangible. In corporate settings mentors are often recognized for their participation in mentoring. Sometimes it's an honor just to be selected as a mentor. And then there's the plaque, the article in the company newsletter, and the awards banquet where the mentors and mentorees are recognized. And mentorees often rise in the organization and come back to take care of their former mentors.

Next-generation mentoring offers none of that. This is a one-way street . . . from mentor to mentoree. No payback. No quid pro quo. Just selfless giving. And it's wonderful.

Our Father in heaven is watching, and selflessness makes Him smile. Of all the human endeavors He likes, mentoring younger ones for kingdom purposes has to be one of His favorites . . . because that's what His Son did when He was here. And we all know how we get drawn into and start to love whatever good things our kids get into and love.

Gratitude

I've spoken about gratitude and the fact that mentors are givers not takers. God puts within His true followers a deep motivation, a true calling. They recognize that there's more to life than this life, and they're motivated in a special way because of this understanding.

Let me explain.

When I surrendered to God in September 1983, I didn't have anything anymore. I had lost my wife and kids. My career had hit a brick wall. I had worshipped the wrong god for years and suddenly realized that it wasn't real or dependable. I was broken.

God had me right where He wanted me. He didn't cause all these bad circumstances to evolve. I had brought all this on myself. And now I was living with the consequences of my decisions and behavior.

God used those tough circumstances to get my attention . . . to reach out to me and say: "I'm here. I love you. I want to help you. With me, you can get through this."

I said, "OK then . . . it's you and me, God. I'm going with you. Whatever you want me to do, that's what I'll do."

I was thrilled to have a real connection . . . a real connection to God. For the first time I began to listen to God instead of just talk at Him. I began to sense His urgings and feel that halt in my spirit when I was acting badly. I started living this reckless life, just loving my wife, my kids, everyone—doing what that "still small voice" led me to do.

God began to bless me. First, my marriage began to work. My kids and I started real relationships. My church life went from going through the motions to real worship. My new business (which I started after leaving the big company where I had hit the wall) began to grow. The discipleship class that we had signed up for became a centerpiece of my spiritual and social life. God gave me the first set of Christian friends I'd ever had. I began to tithe and almost immediately started upping the percentage beyond that minimum.

Year by year, God added more relationships, more depth, more love to my life. And that voice, that connection, that relationship has become my center. God has moved from being a part of my life to being the center of my life. He's my magnetic north. I try not to do anything without thinking about Him and filtering that action through His will for me. When I fail to do that, I fail. Period.

Giving Back

I hear wealthy people talk about "giving back" all the time. Alumni who go on from college to create fortunes, give back to their alma maters with huge donations and endowments. People who start businesses in an area often give back to the communities that fostered their entrepreneurship, locating factories, offices, and distribution facilities in those locations. Those facilities create jobs, pay taxes, and enrich the communities that helped them get started.

Since God has in essence given me my life, what part of it is truly mine?

None.

It's His, all His!

He can take any of it away anytime He wants. So in reality it's His anyway.

How hard is it to be generous with someone else's money? Just watch what your kids order when you take them out to dinner and they know you're paying the tab! That's the way we should look at our lives. They're His. "Lord, how would You have me use my time for You, for Your kingdom?" Don't be surprised if part of the answer isn't mentoring some younger people.

The other dimension to giving as a mentor relates to how you give to your group once you have one.

My most valuable gift to my group is my time and attention. Where in today's world does one go to be heard, where someone genuinely listens with no personal agenda, with nothing to gain or lose? My only motive is to point these guys to Jesus, who is their dependable true mentor.

I can listen objectively and without the pressure of trying to impress, to be smart, or always to be right.

Commitment to "the Cause"

When you look at mentoring in the broadest context, it's always around a cause. When football coaches mentor their young players, it's toward the cause of building a better team and, ultimately, of winning championships. When head coaches mentor their assistants, it's about building a stronger coaching staff that over time goes a long way toward creating a winning tradition.

When corporations create mentoring programs and foster mentoring relationships, it's about the same thing . . . success for the company. We can be more successful as an organization if we leverage the talent and experience of our senior people into the performance of our younger managers. It just makes sense.

Jesus, the world's greatest mentor, did a lot of His mentoring for "the cause." He was totally about His Father's business, demonstrating the nature of God and preparing His mentorees for the task of taking the story of God to the world and to future generations.

Even when He did things that seemed earthly like healing Peter's mother-in-law (see Matt. 8:14–15), it had a purpose beyond the moment . . . beyond the human need . . . beyond His friendship with Peter. He was always thinking, *How can my Father get glory out of this?* I can imagine that healing his wife's mother did a lot to help Peter's wife in dealing with Peter's being gone all the time, traveling around with Jesus. But you can also be sure that Peter's wife was seeing incredible change in her husband, change for the better.

As I've mentored these younger men, their wives have become my champions. While they miss having their husbands home on the nights they're with me, they are more than delighted with the changes they see God making in their husbands.

Even though Jesus spent most of His time with His mentorees, He never put them ahead of His Father and the cause of the kingdom. He would walk away after big events to go pray. Just when you would expect to see the disciples hoisting the cooler full of Gatorade to dump it on His head, Jesus would head off to be with the Father . . . alone with His Dad.

My motivation in creating next-generation mentoring groups has been to encourage and equip younger men to become more godly. Taking a line from my purpose statement, I'm about helping people become all they can be and to give all of themselves to Jesus Christ.

When guys I mentor live lives of character, when they stay married, point their kids to Jesus as they raise them, and succeed in their careers, I believe they say to those around them, "Hey, Christianity may not be all that bad a way to go." And then hopefully God will compel them toward Himself, and they can understand what "the way" really is.

The Dangerous Ego

Jesus knew who He was. He didn't have anything to prove to anyone. He did miracles and wonders to establish His divinity, not to show off or say, "Hey, look at me." He deflected credit for everything He did to the Father, never taking credit Himself.

Mentors like Jesus love to watch their mentorees go beyond themselves . . . to do greater things than they've done.

Peter Drucker was thrilled by the success of his mentoree, Jim Collins, author of *Good to Great* and *Built to Last*. Drucker wrote tons of books and had huge impact on modern business management but never hesitated to help Collins as he shaped his message and business philosophy. Collins wrote:

> I'll never forget asking, "How can I ever pay you back?" and his saying, "You've already paid me back. I've learned so much from our conversation." That's when I realized where Drucker's greatness lay, that unlike a lot of people, he was not driven to say something. He was driven to learn something.
>
> I feel proud that I followed the advice. It's a huge debt. I can never pay it back. The only thing I can do is give it to others. Drucker had said, "Go out and make yourself useful." That's how you pay Peter Drucker back. To do for other people what Peter Drucker did for me.[3]

Great mentors know who they are. They've settled that issue to the degree that it can be settled by any mere mortal. They get great joy in seeing their wisdom, knowledge, and experience live on to help others.

Collins comment about Drucker's listening and learning is huge. When a person knows who he is, he's comfortable in any situation. He doesn't spend energy wondering what the other person is thinking. He can spend all his energy listening and trying to understand.

I've heard horror stories of mentors who were motivated by their ego. Retired executives are especially gifted but often especially egocentric. They've been looked up to . . . sometimes feared . . . for years and years. "They know because they know." But as mentors, they can be too wrapped up in their own successes . . . their own way of doing things.

They forget that Jesus asked questions . . . lots of questions, and He listened. He didn't just talk. On those few occasions when He did, He was intentional about it. It was almost like, "OK fellows, get your pens and write this down" . . . and then He spoke the Sermon on the Mount. But many, if not most, of His parables came as answers to questions.

Jesus tailored His message . . . His answer . . . to the needs of the asker. He didn't just blabber on and on with what He knew.

Thus, the selfless mentor is a good listener, dispensing his wisdom to meet the needs of his mentorees, not his need to tell all that he knows.

That's the selfless heart . . . the God-seeking heart of the mentor.

A Big Surprise

God, who is the perfect Father, loves to give good gifts to his children. Now we can debate all day what a "good gift" is. My suspicion is that it isn't a new car, a big hit in the stock market, or a fancy vacation. And He hasn't given any of those things to me as a result of my mentoring, but He has surprised me with some incredible gifts like notes from guys who thank me for helping them have a better marriage and notes that describe more balanced work lives. They thank me for playing a little part in that. They send pictures of newborn children wrought of marriages that were at one time shaky at best.

Most of all . . . friends. God has turned the guys that I've mentored into my best friends. I never expected that.

Isn't that just like God? To take something you give Him in a selfless way and turn around and give you blessings beyond anything you could imagine?

The Mentoree Perspective from Richard Chancy

When I was in high school, I got to be friends with a young married guy who was actively involved in my youth group. His name was Rocky Jones, and he owned a trophy shop in my hometown. Rocky was great about letting me stop by and just hang with him while he worked. He talked to me about everything from girls to high school to college. We talked about faith and what I wanted to do with my life. He had a boat, and we sometimes went waterskiing. He was just a really good friend and, looking back, was probably one of the most important mentors in my life. Rocky took the time to listen to me and asked really good questions. I now see that God used Rocky to help shape the next few years of my life and really had an impact on who I am today.

A few years ago I got a call that Rocky had a heart attack and passed away. He was forty-two. It never occurred to me that he was only eight years older than me. I spent a lot of time thinking through my memories of him, and I realized something: Rocky had intentionally set out to impact my life for Jesus. He had invested in me for *my* sake and expected nothing in return. I don't think I ever thanked Rocky for all those hours he spent with me, but I don't think he really wanted to be thanked because it wasn't about him. The best "thank-you" I could ever give him would be to do for other guys what he did with me. Because it's not about me either.

Regi helped me understand this during our first one-on-one lunch together. Throughout the year, Regi makes a point to spend some one-on-one time with each guy in the group. I was one of the fortunate ones who had the opportunity to sit down with him early in the year. I think the point was for Regi to get a better idea of how he could use his time to help me.

When he asked me what I thought about the group so far, I said, "Honestly I'm struggling with the group. I'm not getting a lot out of it. I'm not really a "sit at the feet" kind of guy. I said,

"Regi, I'm having a hard time hearing what you're saying because I don't have a level of trust that allows me to accept input from you." I thought I'd knock him off balance with that one. But instead he backed up and began building a bridge with me.

"Mentoring isn't about me, Richard. But you know . . . it isn't about you either. It is about both of us learning to live in a way that honors God."

He told me why he mentors men. He talked about how the first years of his marriage had been so hard on Miriam. Looking back, he felt that a lot of the pain he caused her could easily have been avoided with a little guidance. His greatest desire as a mentor was to honor God by digging in and challenging guys like me to focus on what really matters . . . to avoid the mistakes he made. He talked about the potential he saw in me and the potential obstacles I would face if I didn't make some changes. In a matter of minutes I was able to get over the hump and understand that Regi really was interested in guiding me, and I was ready to listen.

Then, to my surprise, he told me that I didn't appear to be comfortable in my own skin . . . that I almost vibrate with an over-the-top achievement motivation. I don't know that I had ever thought of it in those terms, but I have to admit that he was dead on. I'm fortunate to know where that vibration comes from. It's a self-esteem issue.

My parents named me after a friend who died in Vietnam. His name was Richard William O'Keefe, and he went by the name Dick. My mother was pregnant with me when he died, so when I was born, they named me Richard William and gave me the nickname Dick to honor their friend.

You can't imagine the amount of ridicule I was subjected to as a child. I started calling myself Richard at the age of eight; but living in a small town, nicknames tend to stick with you. As a result I always felt like I was being made fun of . . . like an outsider. And while I am extremely extroverted as an adult, my palms still sweat when I meet new people . . . leftover anxiety from being hung with an embarrassing nickname as a child.

As a result of the damaged self-image from my childhood name, I found myself trying to excel at too many things . . . ever feeling that I wasn't good enough . . . always feeling like I needed to work harder or strive more and be the best at everything.

Regi began to help me understand the concept of being completely and totally accepted by my heavenly Father. He reminded me that I didn't need to strive to be good enough, and in fact no amount of striving would earn what Christ had already offered me. I still vibrate, but my oscillation rate is much lower.

Sometimes the best thing a mentor can do is simply to hold a mirror up in front of you. Regi was willing to talk about what he saw in me even at the risk of offending me. The funny thing about blind spots is that I am the only one blind to my blind spots. But when someone else sees you more clearly than you can see yourself and has the courage to speak truth to you in love, the blind can begin to see again. That's what Regi helped me do.

THE IMPACT OF MENTORING

When you mentor people like me, you aren't just impacting one person or a group . . . you are impacting their families, their friends, and the people they work with. You're impacting who they'll mentor and that circle of influence. It's intergenerational. That was the strategy Christ used. And in reality it's the reason we even know about Him. One person shared with someone else, and that person shared, and the generations continue to share the message of Christ.

I'd like to ask you to stop reading for a few minutes and take out a sheet of paper. Write down the names of the three or four people who have most impacted your faith over the course of your life. Who helped paint your high-level picture of how your belief system developed? If they didn't point you to Christ, they helped you grow closer to Him after you believed.

I'll be willing to bet that you can pinpoint a few people who really invested in you, people who went the extra mile. They helped you experience God in a tangible way. I'm asking you to repay the favor by being that person for a few guys out there who are just like me, to be intentional about investing in other people the way the people on your list invested in you. The return far outweighs the investment.

THE SECRET SAUCE:
A GROUP

Jesus, the world's greatest mentor, worked with a group. That's right, a group.

> All my life, I've thought of mentoring only as an individual thing . . . one-on-one, life on life. But Jesus started . . . and ended . . . with a group.

How could we all have missed that? I can't find a single book or article about mentoring that approaches the process from a group perspective. I guess it's like that dead-looking flower arrangement on my bookshelf. I've seen it so much that I don't see it anymore.

In Christian circles the mentoring paradigm is Paul, Barnabas, and Timothy. We're told, "Everyone should have a 'Paul,' an older, wiser, more mature mentor." "Everyone should have a 'Barnabas,' a peer . . . someone who is 'on mission' with us . . . someone we can share with, have accountability with, do life with." And "everyone should have a 'Timothy,' a younger, less experienced, less mature person we can mentor and pour our life into."

That's a neat picture. And I would love to have that trifecta. I've spoken with a few people who have had it, people who have had individuals playing those exact roles in their lives. They're incredibly blessed, but they are very few.

And it's taken years. Most of those relationships have evolved slowly over time, most often being haphazard and loosely organized. There hasn't been intentionality in either establishing the relationships or fulfilling the mentoring roles with any real dispatch. God just put those people into each other's lives. It just happened.

Several years ago some of us tried to launch a mentoring program at North Point Community Church. We had no trouble drawing a couple of hundred guys who wanted to be mentored. And we drew a pretty good number of potential mentors as well.

The problem came in trying to hook them up. We built a database and tried to match guys by the area of town they lived or worked in. We tried matching them by their college alma mater or by the industry they worked in. We tried everything. Even with the blessing and active participation of Andy Stanley, our senior pastor, it failed to take off.

Why?

Because you can't orchestrate friendship. You can't *make* one-on-one mentoring relationships happen. Sort of like marriage . . . no one can explain or predict how God puts certain people into each other's lives, but He does.

When I look at Jesus, I see intentionality. He didn't have time for His mentorees, His "Timothys" just to show up. He had to go and get them . . . and He did.

He already had His mentor, His "Paul" . . . God the Father Himself!

And there was (and is) no peer to Jesus, so the Barnabas thing was a nonstarter. If anyone was colaboring with Jesus, it would have been John the Baptist. And clearly Jesus had utmost respect for John, asking him to baptize Him and taking on some of His disciples. Jesus knew John's role, and John knew Jesus' role. They were both mentoring their followers for future impact in the kingdom, but there is little recorded collaboration between them.

After the resurrection, Jesus sent for His disciples and said, "Go and tell my *brothers* to go to Galilee" (Matt. 28:10). Brothers. I don't think He'd ever called them that before.

I realize that all relationships are individual . . . you can't have a relationship with a group. It's ultimately one-on-one, both between mentor and mentoree and between mentorees. Just as God doesn't have a relationship with a church; He has individual relationships with each person within the church. But I believe the group context is the "secret sauce" of mentoring on an intentional basis. It can set the individual relationships in motion and even speed up the process of developing trust.

Efficiency

When I was fourteen years old, I landed my first job working in a grocery store, bagging groceries, stocking shelves, and cleaning up.

Each night after closing, someone had to clean the linoleum-floored aisles. To do this, we used these large dust mops. They were heavy, bulky, and a little moist with some sort of wax that had been preapplied.

So on this particular Friday night, I was off with my dust mop, scampering up one side of the aisle and back down the other.

Mr. Cantrell, the store manager, was quite a feared figure to everyone in the store. He didn't smile much, was white haired and red faced . . . not the guy you wanted to cross or disappoint. In my first few weeks on the job, he had spoken to me maybe once or twice.

As I came to the end of the dog food aisle, Mr. Cantrell spotted me. He stopped, turned, and walked directly toward me. I remember the blood rushing out of my legs . . . the way it does when you top a hill going a little too fast and see the police car with the radar gun pointed directly at you. I hardly noticed that he had a dust mop in his hand.

When he got to me, he reached out and took the dust mop from my hand without saying a word. He then took his dust mop and mine, put one in each hand, and proceeded up the aisle, mopping the entire aisle with one pass instead of two. When he reached the end of the aisle, he turned to the next aisle, out of my sight. I quickly turned the other way, rounded the corner just in time to see Mr. Cantrell walking directly toward me with both mops, cleaning the entire aisle in one pass. When he got to me, he stopped . . . handed both dust mops to me, and said, "Work smart, son, and not so hard." I've never forgotten that.

Mentoring in a group is "working smart and not so hard."

Why tell your story eight times to eight people when you can tell it once to all eight at the same time? Why share your successes and failures over and over again when you can share them once for multiple listeners to hear?

Jesus didn't. Time after time He was speaking, teaching, answering questions in front of His group . . . for all to hear and consume. To be sure individuals in the group had different levels of understanding, but they would come back and ask questions to get clarification. "Explain this parable to us," the disciples asked on multiple occasions. Then Jesus would explain it. Once. For all to hear and understand.

One of the biggest reasons men and women don't mentor in the twenty-first century is the amount of time they perceive it takes. Everyone is so busy, the idea of meeting one-on-one with someone . . . time after time . . . meeting after meeting . . . just seems too much. You never know when the need to get together is going to arise. You never know what the issue is going to be, and you wonder if this open-ended commitment has any rational end or if it is going to do any good. But create a group, and it's totally different.

As a mentor I feel like it's worth the investment of time to benefit eight people, much more than if it's just for one. I have the time scheduled a year in advance . . . one night a month, three hours . . . highly efficient. And with e-mail, follow-up conversations, questions, explanations—all that is so incredibly efficient.

As I said earlier, my venture into next-generation mentoring groups was out of self-defense. I couldn't do the number of individual meetings that were needed and keep a job, family, and a brain. So I put the first group together to leverage my time. The time required has been less, the number of people affected has been more, the time required is organized and planned, and the fruit has been far beyond anything I could have ever imagined.

Simpler Structure

When I think about the one-on-one mentoring I've done, I'm reminded of how helter-skelter it felt. Usually, the conversation was driven by the "issue of the day" and didn't get much beyond that. Over the course of a year or two, I'm sure the mentoree got some help and grew in his faith. But did they get my best? Did they get what they wanted but maybe missed out on what they needed?

Everything we do in life is either goal achieving or tension relieving. Issue-driven mentoring isn't intentional from the mentor's perspective. It's reactive, not proactive. It's not directly goal achieving . . . it's tension relieving for the mentoree since he gets help with an issue that's pressing at the time. He either gets some helpful advice, or he gets courage to act on his decision. Misery loves company, and it's comforting to have a respected adviser agree with your plan of action, even if it is *your* plan of action.

And I'm not saying that mentors shouldn't be available for and responsive to the pressing issues of their mentorees. We can't love them and not come to their aid when they're in trouble.

But if all health care were delivered from an ambulance, we certainly wouldn't ever see lives saved through open-heart surgery. No one would ever get a physical . . . there would be no prevention of disease. And if all mentors do is help people in their crisis times, real growth will be slow, and mentors will wear themselves out.

I've found that mentoring a group of guys together, meeting once a month for a year, gives me a simple structure and a measured pace, allowing me to achieve my goals with these guys.

Reduced Pressure on the Mentor

Mentoring in a group environment puts less pressure on the mentor than one-on-one mentoring. The mentor gets to lay out (and control) the agenda. He gets to talk about what he wants to talk about, understanding that a good mentor is going to be responsive to his group and relevant to their issues and needs.

Whenever he's stumped or doesn't have an answer, he can simply turn to the rest of the group and say: "Well, what do you guys think? What would you say to this question?" Not only is he getting himself off the hook for knowing everything, but he's bringing along future mentors as they exercise their ability to give advice in a non-threatening, non"preachy" way.

As a matter of fact, this dynamic of mentorees helping one another was one of the biggest surprises for me as a mentor.

When a guy has an issue, someone in the group usually has experience on that issue. Often someone will speak up and say, "I've been there. Let me tell you what happened to me."

At no time in my mentoring experience have I seen this played out more than when one of my groups "went deep" on marital expectations.

"I work hard . . . I provide well . . . why shouldn't I expect certain things from my wife?" asked Rick. It was late in the evening on our retreat. A couple of the other guys chimed in with agreement. I explained that we're to love our wives as Christ loved the church . . . unconditionally. I reminded them of how Jesus got none of His expectations met by us, by the church, by anyone . . . but He gave Himself up for us anyway. Here's Rick's recollection of that night.

> It was Friday night. We had all eaten a great meal and were sitting down for the last session of the night. Two of us had yet to give our testimony. I was one of them. Boy, I was so nervous. I was going to have to share what I had masked so well for so long. But as I look back now, God was preparing my heart for a night that I would never forget.
>
> My story started with a dysfunctional family life and a broken home, a dad that was never around and a mom that was always at work. I had mastered this self-pity party all my life and didn't expect this night would be any different. But after my attempt to explain my life, my mentor had one question that rocked my world: How is your marriage now? I loaded up and started firing out. I have done all these things. I work hard. I provide. I clean. I help with the kids. Why can't my wife just do something? Why can't she just cut me some slack?
>
> What I didn't realize was that everything coming out of my mouth was what _I_ needed, what _I_ was doing

right, what she was doing wrong. All of my expectations of her were selfish demands by me. As I looked across the room, I could see that several of my peers were agreeing with me. So I felt pretty good. But I was sadly mistaken.

I was told in so many words from my mentor—that I was the one who had it wrong! I was the one that was screwing things up by putting expectations on my wife that she could never live up to, and at the end of the day I would be divorced just like my parents . . . if I didn't change.

About that time, J. D. spoke up. He was the other guy who hadn't yet shared his faith story.

"Regi's right," he said, with his voice breaking. "I know because my constant expectations led my first wife to divorce me."

The room got dead quiet. No one knew that J. D. had been married before. He went on to tell his story. He had such credibility because he was speaking from his heart . . . and his painful personal experience.

In that moment, I told myself and the group that was not going to happen. I had been through that, and I was going to do everything in my power not to let that happen. You see those words again: my power. *Regi reminded me that Jesus puts no expectations on me, on any of us, that He loves us unconditionally. I sat with my face in my hands and realized that he was right. By this time I was mentally exhausted. My mind and heart ached. I asked myself what was I going to do. I'm either going to continue to live this way, or I am going to change now with God's help. So I called my wife; it was 2:30 a.m. I broke down in tears and told her how wrong I had been . . . how I wanted to change. She forgave me, and we started over.*

No End in Sight

It's really hard to visualize how a mentoring relationship ends. I believe that's why it's so hard to motivate more mature people to mentor. They've achieved some success. They enjoy having more control of their time and often become pretty selfish with it. They want to know what they're getting into, how much time it's going to take, and when it will be over. I'm not being judgmental . . . I'm being honest. This is not just assessment . . . this is confession. I ask those questions *every time* I'm asked to get involved in something.

Before I began to do next-generation mentoring groups, young men would ask me to mentor them, and I would think: *I wonder how much time this is going to take? How often is this guy going to call me? When will it be over? Is this mentoring or adult adoption?*

One of my mentors, who was also my pastor for ten years, had the courage to tell me once, "Regi, I think you've learned all you're going to learn from me." It's rare . . . that someone would be honest enough to promote you on to be mentored by someone else.

The beauty of a mentoring group is that it has a defined end.

Most mentoring relationships just peter out over time. Guys stay friends and occasionally communicate, but there isn't a time when it's understood, "OK, you're on your own now. I've given you my best. Go and do your best." Having that defined end is cool, and it's a lot easier to nail that down with a group.

Two-way Street

Another surprise for me as I started mentoring groups of guys came in what *I* was able to learn. I had envisioned teaching them lots of stuff but never counted on learning so much myself.

In selecting sharp young men, I'm getting access to the best and brightest minds of the future. These are men who will lead our businesses, our schools, and our churches. They've read and learned on their own, and their perspectives often stretch mine.

I also learn how their generation sees the world. I'm able to stay abreast of cultural trends and issues through my firsthand involvement in the lives of men who are living it out. They listen to different music, watch different TV shows and movies, and use a different language at times. I'm able to keep up and stay relevant by my involvement with them.

So mentoring isn't just a one-way street from me to them. It's a two-way street, with me gaining valuable insight and useful knowledge from them as well.

Healthy Peer Pressure

Another dimension to mentoring in a group environment is the peer pressure that the guys in the group put on one another.

Because I make such a big deal about being on time, there's an uproar when someone shows up a few minutes late. The guys chastise the late guy big time . . . I don't need to say a thing.

In a recent group one of my mentorees named Jonathan moved during the middle of the year. And he didn't just move across town . . . he moved back to his hometown nine hours away. But he intended to live up to the covenant he made, so he drove back each month to attend our sessions—eighteen hours round-trip!

On his first trip back for our meeting, one of the other guys had been asked by his boss (the CEO of his company) to stay late at work and attend an important long-range planning session. Staying for that meeting would mean missing our mentoring group. He prayed, he pondered, he even called me with his boss standing by the phone, looking for any possible way out . . . from his boss or from me! Neither of us gave in. He was going to have to decide.

He chose to stay at work and miss the mentoring group.

Can you imagine the grief he took at the next meeting? Jonathan, who had driven eighteen hours to live up to his covenant put it to Bryan big time. "Where are your priorities?" he asked. And he had earned the right to challenge Bryan by paying such a heavy price to be at the meeting himself. I sat silently and watched as these two guys mentored each other. That could only happen in a group context.

Facilitation Versus Teaching

Let's face it. Few teachers can hold our attention for half an hour, much less a full hour. Research has proven that we only retain a small percentage of what we hear anyway, with slightly higher retention when we write stuff down.

Next-generation mentoring is a facilitation model . . . not a teaching model. In eight years of group mentoring, I've *never* spoken to any group for as long as thirty minutes.

I've talked about all the advantages of working with a group versus an individual, but many of us think that if it's a group there has to be a teacher. Our "Sunday school" DNA kicks in before we know it, and we start visualizing mentoring as a Sunday school class.

But that doesn't work in this environment.

A great mentor is one who can listen, ask good questions, bring others into the conversation, and tell a relevant story to make a point. He lets the conversation run when it's going in a good direction but cuts it off as soon as it loses its point.

George Pratt, one of my mentorees, put it this way:

> A mentor is much different from a teacher. Teachers have specific points to share while mentors guide. Our mentor invested his time to find out where we were coming from and then gave practical guidance on areas of growth. Our next-generation mentoring group was never about abstract ideas but about putting things into practice. Whether it was developing a mission statement, listening to God, being intentional with our time in reaching out to others, loving our wives, or raising our children, everything we learned had practical application, which was key to making change.

That's a facilitator, not a teacher.

The Group within the Group

Almost from the outset, I noticed something happening in my next-generation mentoring groups that was unexpected and troubling. I found myself liking a couple of guys a little more than the others. They seemed to "get it" in a special way. When they shared what they'd learned from the book assigned that month, they seemed to have gone a little deeper, thought about it a little more, and presented a more powerful application of what was to be learned.

These guys would ask the best questions, and when I would answer, I'd watch them write stuff down in their notebooks. They always had their homework. They were always on time. They could quote the assigned Scriptures without a hiccup.

But more than all that, I just seemed to love them, and they seemed to love me a little more than the others. They expressed a deeper sense of gratitude for what they were getting and what I was investing in them. Toward the end of the year, they would start telling their friends, "Hey, you've got to apply for this next-generation mentoring group that Regi Campbell does. It'll change your life!"

This "group within the group" has become a fixture. Every year for eight years (and I'm sure it'll happen again this year), one, two, or three of the mentorees are special. They just get it at a deeper level, and they and I develop a deeper bond than the others in the group. Years after these groups graduate, these group-within-the-group guys stay in touch, pray for me, and keep me involved in their lives to some degree.

At first, I felt really guilty for letting this happen. How could I end up favoring one guy over another? This is not democratic . . . heck it many not even be American!

But when I realized the similarities between the next-generation mentoring that I was doing and the practices of Jesus as He mentored the twelve, I knew it was OK.

Jesus had the "big three"—Peter, James, and John. They were His group within the group.

We don't really know how they got to be so special. Luke describes how they were the first ones selected by Jesus . . . how Jesus got into Peter's boat and directed him to a boatload of fish, and then recruited Peter and his friends, James and John, to become "fishers of men." But somehow it's hard to believe that they became so special to Jesus just because they were first. He kind of shot that theory down when He said something about the first being last.

We know that their unique status wasn't necessarily based on their performance, since Peter denied he even knew Jesus and denied Him multiple times. James and John, acting on their apparent need for status and power, asked Jesus if they could be His number one and number two guys. We know the other disciples were indignant over their power grab, and we can assume that Peter was in the group who resented their actions.

I believe these three . . . the group within the group . . . were different because of their love for Jesus.

We know how much Jesus loved John. John was referred to as "the one that Jesus loved," and His love was uniquely demonstrated when, from the cross, He entrusted His mother, Mary, into John's care.

We know little about James, John's older brother, other than we know he had a lot of passion, albeit misplaced at times. Jesus referred to James and John as the "Sons of Thunder" (Mark 3:17). And Scripture tells us that James was martyred, the first of the disciples to die. Moreover, he was martyred by Herod himself, telling us that he must have been creating some pretty high-profile problems with his teaching and preaching.

I also think that Jesus saw Peter, James, and John as having the highest potential.

Peter had embarrassed himself with his bold promises of loyalty only to be followed hours later with his denial of Jesus. But Peter had also gotten out of the boat to walk on the water. Somehow Jesus saw enough potential in Peter that He chose him to head up the church, changing his name from Simon to Peter, which meant "the rock."

Obviously Jesus had seen similar potential in James and John. John wrote a significant part of the New Testament, more than anyone other than Luke and the apostle Paul. John outlived the others and became the patriarch of the movement before his death.

When the disciples are listed in the book of Acts, James is listed second, just after the leader, Peter. This could have reflected James's leadership but could also have reflected his seniority to his younger brother, John.

James and John, the "sons of thunder," along with Peter were clearly Jesus' group within the group.

John McArthur wrote:

> He (James), Peter, and John were the only ones Jesus permitted to go with him when he raised Jairus's daughter from the dead (Mark 5:37). The same group of three witnessed Jesus' glory on the Mount of Transfiguration (Matt. 17:1). James was among the

four disciples who questioned Jesus privately on the
Mount of Olives (Mark 13:3). And he was included
again with John and Peter when the Lord urged the
three to pray with him privately in Gethsemane
(Mark 14:33). So as a member of the small inner
circle, he was privileged to witness Jesus' power in the
raising of the dead, he saw his glory when Jesus was
transfigured, he saw Christ's sovereignty in the way
the Lord foretold the future to them on the Mount of
Olives, and he saw the Savior's agony in the garden.[4]

MacArthur goes on to say that these three were specially prepared so that their faith would be strong in light of their future
suffering and the martyrdom they would face.

What's really cool is that I've never sensed any jealousy or ani-
mosity from the other guys in the group when the "group within the
group" emerges. I guess that validates, at least for me, that it's a God
thing.

Blessings Back to the Mentor

As I said in the beginning, I'm not a theologian . . . not a Bible
scholar. But I do know that one of the great mysteries of Jesus was that
of being fully human and at the same time fully God.

When I consider the four major events that MacArthur alludes
to, I can see the human Jesus wanting some companionship. Having
Peter, James, and John there with Him in His most glorious moment
(when He was transfigured), at one of His most amazing moments
(when He raised the girl from the dead), at one of His most important moments (when He revealed the future to them on the Mount
of Olives), and in one of His darkest moments, when He asked them
to keep watch as He prayed for a way out in Gethsemane. All four of
these were highly emotional times for Jesus the man. Who better to
be there with Him than His closest friends?

As I look at my life today, those closest to me . . . those whose
presence I most enjoy in times of joy, challenge, accomplishment, and
of sorrow . . . are those guys whom I have invested in.

And God has surprised me by using these guys to bless me and
my family in ways only He could have envisioned and engineered.

If you want genuine friends who will be there for life . . . guys God will use to bless you beyond belief, then pull together a next-generation mentoring group. Invest selflessly in a group of high-potential guys. You'll love them, and they'll love you back. Watch what God will do through you, and then don't be surprised when He uses those guys to bless you with love and companionship.

The Mentoree Perspective from Richard Chancy

This morning I had breakfast with one of the guys from my mentoring group that I'm really close to. We were talking about his life story, which he shared with us during the fourth month of next-generation mentoring. He made a major mistake in his marriage early on, and the only person who knew about it was his wife. He talked about how good it felt to share that struggle with the other guys. I could tell that he found freedom in his confession. For the rest of us, it just added momentum to the level of transparency we were developing during this time.

His story also confirmed in my mind that, as men, we struggle with the same things: the need to be respected and admired, intimacy with our wives, and intimacy with Christ. We struggle with purity, greed, and pride. And we feel constant stress to leave a legacy and to know that our lives really matter.

The irony is that so many of us struggle alone when the guy right next to us might have been where we are. But we won't engage.

Why then do we try to do it alone?

I think it is always pride. Do we really think we can do this alone? To ask for help is as weak as asking for directions. *I'll figure it out*, we think.

But willpower only takes us so far, and when it fails, the loneliness is awful. As Thoreau said, "Most men lead lives of quiet desperation." In the end, isolation is a choice. Coming out of it may be painful, but you are either coming out or going deeper into isolation at any given time. The choice is yours.

As a mentor you have the opportunity to create environments that destroy the walls of isolation for men. It's what I call a disruptive environment. Once we taste what true intimacy with other people is like, it begins to grow into every area of our lives.

That is the critical thing Jesus understood about investing in the disciples. He knew how difficult their path would be after He was gone, and He knew they wouldn't be capable of doing it alone. So He gave them the gift of brotherhood . . . guys with a common vision and passion. They never went out in the world alone; they were always in groups of at least two. They lived in relationship with one another. And they understood those relationships were crucial to the success of their mission.

Writing this chapter has been especially difficult for me because, looking back, I see how I could've really learned a lot more from the guys in my group. Part of me feels like I missed out on some valuable lessons by not being more open to hearing these guys speak into my life. I have a tendency to take pride in the mountains I've already climbed. I don't usually talk about what I'm struggling with right now. It's really a false sense of transparency.

On our retreat weekend I made the comment that I didn't know if listening to a sermon was the right place for a mature believer to be on a Sunday morning. Honestly, I didn't really mean to bring this up because I hadn't worked it out on my own yet. It was, however, something that I was struggling with at the time. The struggle was created by a feeling that I was the guy who shows up on Sunday at church always asking to be fed but wasn't willing to feed anyone else. I was struggling with acting on what I claimed to believe. But my accidental portrayal of my struggle came across as my issuing a challenge to the group.

The guys unleashed both barrels on me, letting me know that church was central part of the Christian life and citing all the reasons I was out of line. The conversation went on for quite some time until most of the guys were exhausted.

A wiser man would have taken that debate on from an objective point of view. A guy that was really interested in working out his issues would have made his point and listened to the feedback in an effort to find some clarity on his struggle.

I, on the other hand, went into debate mode and argued my point as if I was sold out on it, mostly to save face. I tend to take the opposite point of view for argument's sake even if I have not bought in to it.

When it was over, Regi was ready to throw me into the ocean. A couple of the guys came back to me afterwards to check and make sure I was all right, but I hadn't even been phased by it. I missed an opportunity to find some clarity that would take me another year to sort out.

That just proves how much I need relationships with other men. I need connection and transparency and heavy doses of guidance. I think we all need those things. Some men, however, are so wounded they can't climb over the mountain of their own brokenness, so they stay disconnected and isolated. There are guys who will continue to wear a mask and not ever be known truly by another living soul, unless someone comes along and challenges them to pry the mask loose.

The Group within the Group

The group within the group took on an interesting context during our year of mentoring. I truly did feel like one of the guys in that smaller group. It wasn't exactly what I would consider the select group but more of a group of guys who needed the most help and were willing to accept direct feedback on our weaknesses. Regi came at me pretty hard on several occasions, and I didn't run away. Even when my pride took one on the chin, I knew it was best for me to be able to internalize what he was saying. As a mentor, you may make your biggest impact in the guys who are most willing to accept their need for change. Just about everyone wants some sort of change in his life, but only a few are willing to sacrifice to have it.

4

HANDPICKED FOR HISTORY

We don't know how Jesus went about picking His mentorees. We have eyewitness reports of people who were there when He popped the question but not much more.

We know that He had a lot more than twelve to choose from, but how did He decide?

And why twelve? Why *that* twelve? How did He decide whom to pick and whom not to pick?

And what can we learn about whom we pick, or how many, from what Jesus did?

Let's address the easy one first . . . the "how many" question.

The Right Number Is . . .

We're about big. More. More is always better than less.

Churches, maybe more than any other institution, are always focused on "how many." If it's not big numbers, it's not working. If the numbers aren't getting bigger, then something's wrong.

This is rooted in our doubts about our faith. We think, *If more people are doing what we're doing, believing what we're believing, then the chances are greater that we're right and not stupid.* But that's just an opinion.

How did Jesus decide that His "church," His group of insiders, would be only twelve? Sure, there were others. But the twelve were pretty much it.

The Pharisees and Sadducees consistently drew large crowds, but it was the law. You had to be there. But Jesus . . . He didn't seem to be into that. He was working with the twelve, and if others wanted to come along or listen in, that was OK. Sometimes the crowd seems to have been relatively small. At other times it swelled to thousands.

I can only guess at how Jesus landed on twelve as the number of disciples based on my own experience. In my first mentoring group, I picked ten guys. I wanted to have eight, and I had narrowed the field down to eight. I just felt that in one year, I could really get to know each of the guys in a group of eight, and they could get to know one another. Unlike Jesus, where He lived and traveled with His guys 24-7, I would be seeing these guys and interacting with them only once a month. And Jesus was looking at three years of mentoring . . . I was thinking in terms of only one.

Did I mention that I mentored ten guys the first year, even though I wanted to only have eight?

Why? you might ask.

The answer . . . I didn't have the guts to say no to the other two. I should have. As a matter of fact, the two guys who grew the least and were least committed to the process were the two guys I added because I didn't have the courage to say no.

You see, we don't have any record of Jesus' turning down any applicants for "disciple of Jesus Christ." We know that He had many followers. We know that He prayed long and hard before He made His selections. We assume that any number of His followers would have said yes to the opportunity to become one of Jesus' inner circle, learn to heal people and do miracles, and potentially sit at the right hand of the next king of the Jews (as they saw it at the time).

Picking Potential

You see, I believe Jesus chose the twelve men that God wanted Him to pick. He was twelve for twelve. He batted a thousand!

How can I say that even in light of the fact that He had one betrayal, one who denied his affiliation with Jesus, eleven who ran away when Jesus was arrested, and two who were jockeying for favored-son status. Even after doing hundreds of miracles, being killed and coming back to life, one of His mentorees doubted that He was really alive. What a group!

There were the three whom Jesus clearly connected with more meaningfully than the others—Peter, James, and John. Why didn't Jesus just pick nine more like them?

So much of what Jesus did had at least two purposes. He was mentoring the disciples for their future role in taking the story of Jesus and the truth of His kingdom to the world. That part is clear, but Jesus was also using these people . . . these situations, to construct the message in the Bible . . . a dual purpose.

Rob Bell, in his book *Velvet Elvis*, tells us that the men selected by Jesus to be His disciples (mentorees) were basically rejected as future disciples by the Jewish rabbis of their day. Every young man learned the Torah up to the age of twelve or thirteen, but then only the brightest, most righteous were selected to become disciples and continue to higher learning and ultimately to become rabbis themselves. Bell says that the fact that most of the disciples were fishermen and laborers tells us they were not invited to become disciples of the established rabbis.

This can at least partially explain the seemingly irrational response the disciples had when Jesus, who was kind of a "rock-star" rabbi, said to Peter, James, and John, "Follow me," and they dropped their fishing nets and went. Having been relegated to failure status in the local Jewish hierarchy, they jumped at the chance to become disciples of rock-star rabbi Jesus.

Taking Them to the Next Step

It's always mystified me how Jesus, who was God in a human body, could have/would have picked Judas as a disciple. If He could see Phillip under the tree hours before He saw him in person, you know Jesus could see where Judas was going to end up. Yet He not only chose him . . . He washed his feet just hours before he betrayed Him.

Why?

First, Jesus knew that He would leave us with the challenge of "in the world but not of the world." We know that we are made in the image of God but that our job here on Earth is to reflect the image of God, to be like Jesus. Had Jesus picked the "Brady Bunch" for disciples and no one had ever really messed up, how credible would His message of acceptance, tolerance, and love be? Through His interaction with Judas, Jesus put action to the words of "love your enemies" . . . up close and personal.

Another reason was that Judas fulfilled an important function. He was the CPA of the ministry, and every ministry needs a good CPA. We've so sanitized the story of Jesus that we've omitted some of the elements that confirm its truth. We don't know how Jesus and His mentorees sustained life over the three and a half years of their engagement. But we know that there was cash in the account at the end, and Jesus probably picked Judas, at least in part, because he was a competent treasurer.

But maybe more important, Jesus told us that He was doing the work of the Father. His Father, God, does His work in people individually, one step at a time. Jesus handpicked His disciples, and we see how they grew, one step at a time. We can see that growth in Peter, James, and John pretty easily. It's a little harder to see it in some of the other guys, like Thomas, who doubted even what he was seeing with his own eyes. He eventually came around.

But Judas probably grew as well. He just missed a few things. And before you get too self-righteous and judgmental, look at some other folks who've missed a few things—like Martha, who was serving so hard she missed the intimacy of Jesus. I'm not disputing her faith . . . just stating what Jesus said in Luke 10 . . . that Mary chose "what is better" or "the best part" . . . intimacy through grace versus works (Martha).

I believe that Judas was caught up in the movement with Jesus. He came too far and went through too much not to have been. But getting caught up in the movement might have led to a zeal for the movement over a zeal for Jesus. Ever know anyone so zealous for their church that they forgot about Jesus? Or someone so zealous for their company that they forgot about the customers that made their company great?

Judas could have become zealous for the good that could be done by Jesus, (establishing an earthly kingdom [his idea] versus an invisible kingdom [Jesus' idea]) that he couldn't deal with the frustration of not having it happen his way. We've made Judas into an icon for betrayal. Yet there are "whistle blowers" all around us . . . people who instigate church splits, and those who throw preachers and church leaders under the bus every day. We often call them "brave."

I believe Judas's growth exploded after the crucifixion. He realized the difference between the movement of Jesus and the truth of Jesus. I can visualize his remorse over Jesus' death and how he must have felt about what he had done. But I can also imagine him beginning to remember what Jesus had said . . . how Jesus had predicted His death and resurrection *before* Judas had betrayed Him. He might have heard that he wasn't the only one who had lost faith. Maybe he heard about Peter's denying Jesus, and about how the others had run away and hidden as well. I can visualize Judas in an intense conversation with God, confessing his mistake, begging forgiveness. Broken. Just where Jesus would have wanted him to be . . . ready to be used in a powerful way.

Imagine the testimony that Judas could have had. Judas: "I betrayed the Lord into the hands of the Romans. They killed Him, but He rose from the dead and forgave me." We know Jesus' response to Peter, even after he denied Him three times. Imagine how awesome Jesus' response to Judas would have been.

But whenever someone hits a spiritual growth spurt, guess who is going to show up?

The devil.

Yep, the evil one is all over someone who is getting closer to the Savior. And that's what happened to Judas. I can just hear what Satan was whispering to Judas. "You're the reason this happened. This is all your fault. You need to take yourself out." And Judas participated in the ultimate pity party and killed himself.

But why is this story important when it comes to picking people to mentor?

Because you're doing the work of the Father, just like Jesus. You're going to pray over your potential mentorees, and God is going to lead you to pick a handful. You're going to meet them right where they are. And you're going to help them take their next step, whatever that next step is for them. I'm only responsible for giving them my best. They (and God) are responsible for what they do with it and for the outcome.

I have a goal that none of the guys I mentor will ever get a divorce. So far . . . in eight years . . . none have. But I have no control over that. I can only give my best shot, pray, and be available to coach them if I get the chance. God is about outcomes . . . I'm about obedience. I pray, love, serve, and trust God for what happens.

The Opposite of Rejection

When I handpick mentorees, I have to deal with the reality that I *didn't* pick others. That's tough, particularly in light of the church's penchant toward "more, more, more."

Think of one program in the church where you can't just sign up. There are few. Generally, if you want to sign up for something, you're in. It may be "first come, first served" and everyone can't get in because of space or personnel limitations, but it's rare in today's church.

Chris, who was in my third group, says about being "handpicked":

> I felt like you had taken the time to pray through whether God was showing you that you could help me grow. If it was just some 'submit application—first eight received are accepted,' it would not have had the same impact.

Another of my guys, David, adds, "Without that handpicking, I might have felt like a burden. I would have struggled with acceptance by the group and by you."

J. D., another of my mentorees, says:

> As I grew up, I was active in sports. My sport of choice
> became soccer, and I became a decent player. Several
> times in my career I had to try out for traveling/select
> teams, and each time I was selected. The idea of
> being selected in a tryout was always a great feeling.
> However, there were two times it really felt good to
> make a team. Both times I was hand selected by the
> coach just to try out. Once you made the team, it was
> a feeling that is hard to describe, and I had not felt it
> in my adult life until next-generation mentoring. It is
> a feeling of value, a feeling of election, selected by one
> that in your eyes is greater than you.

Connected to Your Purpose

Why would you choose a person to mentor? What criteria exist?
What's the model?

Jesus showed us at least three purposes with His disciple picks.

First and foremost, I believe He picked guys for their kingdom
potential. As I said earlier, His results were astounding . . . eleven guys
. . . two billion Christians.

Were they the most talented? Most spiritual? Obviously not.
They had been passed over by the rabbis. Their religious training had
ceased while others had been selected for more. But somehow, Jesus
saw their potential. They followed Him with unwavering loyalty until
the very end. They listened. They practiced what He taught them.
They asked questions.

These mentorees knew about the coming Messiah and His purpose . . . to establish the kingdom of God with the people of Israel.
When they saw Jesus perform miracles, raise people from the dead,
turn water to wine, they wanted to be a part of what He was doing.

Once Jesus pointed out how blessed they were . . . to be eyewitnesses to what the Father was doing through Him, He reminded
them that later generations wouldn't get to see what they were seeing.
He wanted them to grasp, to comprehend, what they were seeing—its
significance and its meaning.

When I pick men for my next-generation mentoring groups, I try to find guys with a vision for their lives. I'm actually happy if their vision is all messed up. That's where I can add value.

Pete was in my first group. A rough-and tumble-Russian immigrant, Pete wrote, "I see myself with a net worth of one hundred million dollars."

He was in. He's exactly the kind of guy I want to engage with. Why?

Because I spent the first twelve years of my work life mindlessly chasing after a goal that I hadn't really thought through. I wanted to go "as far up the ladder (the management hierarchy of AT&T) as fast as I can." Pete, like me, had never really thought about what that meant. What would he do with that much money? How would it help him be a better husband and father? How could it be used to further the kingdom? It was just a number.

Because I know my purpose and have had the experience of living both with and without it, I can help younger guys think through what they're spending their lives for. And since my purpose is to glorify God, hopefully I can help them toward that same purpose.

The approach I've used to help me pick my mentorees involves asking each guy to write his obituary notice for the newspaper. Steven Covey popularized this exercise in his book *Seven Habits of Highly Effective People*. Here is the e-mail I use to assign the candidates the task of preparing their obituary.

> From among you thirteen guys, eight will be in next year's next-generation mentoring group. The next thing I am asking you to do to help me finalize the group is a short writing assignment. Here it is.
>
> Write the obituary announcement that you would like to see in the paper the day after your death (of old age and by natural causes). Write it in the third person, like a reporter. Include the following:
> - Significant professional accomplishments—what would you like the paper to say you accomplished in your professional life?
> - Community accomplishments

- *Church accomplishments*
- *Family accomplishments*
- *A quote from your wife*
- *A quote from each of your children (present and/ or future dreamed-of children)*
- *A quote from your best friend*
- *Finish this paragraph and include it somewhere in your obituary: "In 200X he participated in a mentoring program. It was a significant deal because. . . ."*

That's it. If you are bone dry on doing this but want to, just read some of the obituaries in the paper, and you can get the hang of it. Let's keep it relatively short—no more than a couple of pages, maybe 250 words max. Again, if you have doubts about making the commitment to the group or if you just don't have a peace about this, obey God's voice and opt out. No hard feelings, honest!

The obituary as described here is a sort of vision statement, a way to look inside the head of the candidate and see what he sees for himself and his family in the future. Reviewing each obituary, you get a sense for what is important for this man and where his priorities are. Through a thoughtful review of the obituaries, I select the eight people that I will invest in for the year.

I'm looking for future leaders because God chose to equip me to be a leader. I believe God can leverage my investment through leaders more than followers. So I try to pick guys who are missiles, even if they aren't *guided* missiles. As they say, you can't steer a parked car. So I'm looking for guys who are in motion . . . movers . . . guys who want to grow, to do something big, to make a difference.

Now are you ready for this one? From among the "missiles," I try to eliminate the candidates who seem to have the most mature, well-balanced view of their future. They have less need to be mentored. I try to pick the least mature, most needy future leaders because they are the people I may be able to help the most.

Don't Let Them Pick You

Jesus picked the twelve. They didn't pick Him.

This is one of the most valuable lessons we take from Jesus. And one of the most countercultural aspects of becoming a mentor like Jesus.

Over and over I hear of young people seeking out mentors. "Could you have breakfast with me? I'd like to pick your brain if I could." We've all been there.

The Scriptures don't depict Jesus' mentoring that way. As a matter of fact, we can visualize the rich young ruler as he approached Jesus. He might have been saying, and I'm paraphrasing, "I've been cool. I've obeyed the commandments. What would it take for me to join up, to follow you, to become one of your inner circle?"

We can imagine Jesus . . . reading the young man's motives from his expression of interest in the kingdom: "Great, go sell all your possessions and come back to see me."

End of conversation.

I'm not saying that every young person who seeks out a mentor has wrong motives . . . or even selfish motives. But we can be sure they have *multiple* motives. Proverbs 16:2 says, "All the ways of a man are clean in his own sight, but the LORD weighs the motives" (NASB). That's with an S . . . plural.

Yes, that young man may want advice about how to live for God, but he may also want to access the mentor's network of friends or financial backers. He may want to be known as "a friend of _____, who owns _____ or is CEO of _____." So status could be a motive. He may see the potential mentor as a financial backer for a business idea or as someone who can help him get ahead in his career with good business advice.

I love that Proverbs verse because it reminds me that God loves me even though I do have multiple motives. I bought an antique scale for my office to remind me that I'll always have multiple motives for the things I do. But I desperately want my "God motives" to be at the top . . . to win out over the other ones.

When I pick the guys for my group, they are *my* idea. Led by God, through prayer, I make those decisions.

I've made mistakes on this one, too. When I was putting my first group together, I had picked eight guys and was ready to launch when a former employee called. "Regi," she said, "my husband is in such need of a mentor. Please let him join your group."

I knew that I wanted an even number of mentorees so that I could pair them up (like Jesus did). So adding her husband meant I had to add yet another guy. So the group went from eight to ten.

> Guess which guys gained the least from the group.
> Guess who was late. Guess who liked to talk more
> than listen. Good guess.

Now I subscribe to the axiom of "never form a principle based on your own experience." But when I look at Jesus' proactive approach, when I look at the success of the groups I've led since that first one, I'm convinced that I should pick them and they shouldn't pick me. Guys who are interested apply for the mentoring program, and then I select my guys from the applicants.

Jesus had many disciples. I believe He considered all those potential "applicants" but picked His twelve of His own volition, not theirs.

Seek No Advice

When Jesus picked His mentorees, He sought only the advice of His heavenly Father. We know that He prayed all night long before making His choices, which is the longest prayer time the Bible records. This was a serious decision, and Jesus gave it the time it deserved.

But He didn't interview the candidates. We don't know how much interaction He had with each one before He picked them, but we do know that He went deep with the Father about these decisions. It doesn't seem that He checked any references either. He picked the twelve that His Father led Him to. Period.

It's a daunting task to look at the obituaries of fifteen or sixteen guys and decide which eight I'll mentor. One or two always want to get together to learn more about next-generation mentoring or to differentiate themselves from the other candidates. I always turn down these requests. I don't want to be influenced by personal chemistry, one way or the other. I want to pick the guys that God leads me to . . . not those whom I might enjoy the most.

Jesus ignored the religious status of His mentorees, and so do I. It makes no difference to me when a potential mentoree makes reference to being an elder or a deacon in his church. I don't consider educational accomplishments, economic status, or even reputation. I'm about helping each one become a more godly man, living the God life. So I want to meet each guy right where he is and help him move forward.

I don't check references. I don't talk to people who know these guys. If someone recommends a guy for my group, I simply have the potential mentoree send an e-mail to me. I hold on to that e-mail and directly invite him to apply when I start the process the next year.

The principle here is to let God put the group together. By allowing Him to lead, by not letting it become a beauty contest or a personality match, I'm more dependent on Him to include and exclude the guys He wants me to mentor.

Commitment Required

Now don't get me wrong . . . I use my brain in this process, but it's more to assess the commitment and teachability of a mentoree. When I invite guys to apply for my next-generation mentoring group, they sign a covenant that includes this provision:

> I understand that I am committing to attending every meeting and retreat, being there on time, and having my work done. No exceptions, unless *providentially* hindered. I understand and agree that I will have to say no to important things in order to meet this commitment, and I am willing to do so. We will lay out our schedule for the year at our first meeting. I will manage my other commitments around the dates that are selected for mentoring group meetings and retreats.

That is commitment!

When Jesus invited Peter, James, John, Matthew, and the others, He asked for commitment. The fishermen dropped their nets. The tax collector left his booth. They followed . . . with incredible commitment.

Jesus called His followers to that kind of commitment. Remember when Jesus called the man to follow Him. But the man said, "I will follow you, Lord; but first let me go back and say goodbye to my family" (Luke 9:6 NIV). Remember when Jesus told the story of the guy who said, "Let me first go and harvest my crops . . . then I will come follow you?" And another who said, "First let me go and bury my father" (Matt. 8:21 NIV). Jesus was unbending. When He used the word "first," He said, "Seek *first* His kingdom, and His righteousness, and all these things will be added to you" (Matt. 6:33 NASB), He meant it. Jesus wants total commitment, and it may start for eight younger men in your mentoring group!

That kind of commitment has disappeared from the landscape of "church world" in our times. But it's one of the keys to the success of next-generation mentoring.

Teachability is the other key dimension.

I believe Jesus handpicked His mentorees because they were teachable. They weren't brainwashed into the religious system of their day; otherwise they would have already been disciples of some other rabbi.

These were common men with common sense. They were lay people, just like Jesus. They were ready to learn, and Jesus saw that in them.

As I select my mentorees each year, I confront them with this challenge, again as a part of the covenant they sign:

> I understand that I will be given tough, 'off target' feedback. I will do all within my power to receive this feedback in love and to learn from it. I will avoid defensiveness, knowing that when I defend, I lose the opportunity to learn. I am committing to being open to examine myself; my personality, my past, my habits, my anger, and my responses to people. I want to learn. I want to change, to be more like Jesus Christ in every fiber of my being.

There are James and John, walking down the road behind Jesus, arguing about who will be the greatest in the coming kingdom. Jesus confronts them about their grandiose plans and tells them that if they wish to be great they have to become servants.

In hardheaded, less teachable men, that would have set them off. They would have "exited stage left." But they listened. They stayed in the game. And we know that John did become a servant, taking on the responsibility of serving Jesus' mother after the crucifixion.

We'll go deep on the covenant in chapter 10, but the mentoree I most want to invest in is one who is both committed and hungry to learn . . . not lukewarm know-it-alls.

Let me review. Jesus handpicked His mentorees, and I believe you should too. He picked them with the singular input of His Father. He picked them based on their potential, their commitment, and their teachability. He connected them with His purpose in life, to preach the gospel to the world so that they "may have life, and have it to the full" (John 10:10).

I mentor because I love Jesus and I'm grateful for what He's done for me. I've found the God life that is so meaningful and fulfilling. I have a purpose for living, and I want my mentorees to have nothing less.

The Mentoree Perspective from Richard Chancy

Four years ago a friend of mine who had been part of next-generation mentoring recommended me for mentoring the next year. I spent time preparing and pouring over my obituary. I also decided to submit my life plan, a document I had developed over time detailing my strengths, weaknesses, developmental goals, etc. I jumped through all the hoops and felt like I was ready to start the mentoring year.

Then I got the e-mail from Regi that I hadn't been picked. That was a shocker for me. I'd spent most of my life crafting myself to stand out above the crowd. Not being picked was certainly a blow to my pride, but I processed it and put the idea aside for the time being.

The next couple of years were really fast paced for me. I was beginning a new division of the company I was working for, and that required me to travel much more than I had any previous year.

For the next two years when I got the e-mail to apply for next-generation mentoring, it didn't seem like a good season to make the commitment, so I didn't apply. I continued to read and grow on my own. God had also begun to birth in my heart a question about the life He wanted for me and for us as believers. I began to have a sense that I was settling for something far less than what He wanted for me.

At the end of 2006, I once again received the invitation from Regi. My wife, Kristy, and I spent time talking about the time commitment involved, and we agreed to make the sacrifice if I was selected. So I began the process again. I rewrote my obituary and jumped through all of the hoops, but this time I left out my life plan and anything else that he hadn't asked for. A few months went by and I found out that I had been selected to be in next-generation mentoring group seven. I have to tell you, I was pumped. I think I may have appreciated next-generation mentoring more for having had to work so hard to get in.

I think the whole experience of being passed over has helped me realize the true value and importance of being mentored. Regi saw something in me the second time around that led him to believe that now his time would be effectively spent with me. I knew that he had gone through the process of determining where his time would be best spent. He then determined time invested in me would have a greater impact than time invested with one of the men who weren't chosen. It challenged me to know that, just as I had been passed over for someone else before. Now someone was being passed over for me. That created a lot of weight behind what it meant to be selected.

I'm always fascinated by how I see God working as I look in the rearview mirror. Based on where I was several years ago, there would have been no way for me to have benefited from this process as I did by having to wait a few years.

The point I want you to understand here is this . . . don't worry about the guys you have to leave behind. If you make yourself available to do God's work through mentoring, trust that He puts you with the right guys. Regi told me later that, based on all the information I sent in, he didn't know if he could add value to me. In reality, he was exactly right. I had to move back a little before I was ready to move forward. Don't interfere with what God is doing by trying to force mentoring unless you know a man is ready.

5

STARTING NOW,
ENDING THEN

As I mentioned earlier, several years ago we tried to launch a mentoring ministry in our church. We pulled together a couple hundred men, intending to connect the younger to the older . . . the less mature with the more mature.

As we solicited these more senior men to be mentors, questions kept coming up: What am I getting into? How long is this going to go on? What kind of commitment am I making here?

A lot of guys shied away because we couldn't answer those questions, and I don't blame them. "You're asking me to agree to be a mentor, which I don't know how to do. Then you're asking me to sign up to mentor someone I don't know. You can't tell me how much time it's going to take. And you can't tell me how long this is going to go on!"

That's a hard sell.

I've found there's incredible value in setting a specific beginning and ending date for mentoring. Sure, the relationships will continue after that time, but they come naturally . . . and the mentoring happens as a natural outgrowth of that relationship.

When we look at Jesus, we see that He only mentored His disciples for about three years, so there must be some value in mentoring for a defined period of time. Jesus could have left the carpenter shop any time He wanted. He could have started teaching and mentoring at twenty-eight instead of thirty . . . or even at twenty-five. We know that He was hanging with the best of scholars at twelve years old, so He knew what He was talking about. And if you think about it from an earthly perspective, He was an incredible mentor to be only thirty.

Jesus began His mentoring when He solicited Andrew and Simon (Peter). Then He recruited James and John from their father's fishing business. To these four, He added Matthew and the others. We don't know how old these men were, but we know that they entered into an intense, focused mentoring experience when they "dropped their nets" and followed Jesus. It started with "follow Me" and ended with "it is finished" . . . or so they thought.

When Do You Start?

I believe we overly complicate the job of mentoring. When you're thirty, you can mentor twenty-year-olds. When you're twenty-five, you could potentially be a fabulous mentor to an eighteen-year-old. But when do you start? How do you know it's time?

Again, we look at Jesus.

He's there at a wedding, accompanied by some of His friends and followers. His mom comes to Him in a panic. "The hosts are out of wine, and the party's just started. Do something, Jesus!"

Jesus was reluctant. He told His mom, "My time has not yet come" (John 2:4).

He wasn't sure that it was time to start His ministry. We don't know why He wasn't sure, and to guess about it flies right into the mystery of Jesus' being fully man and fully God at the same time.

As a human Jesus could have been afraid. He had known for a long time that He was special, that He was here for a unique purpose. But in the moment, when He's confronted publicly with *starting something He's never done,* there's a pause. Not that He would even think about backing out or backing down. Still, stepping into the role of miracle worker, Messiah, Son of God, had to be daunting.

The Father put Him in that situation, and in that moment He responded. He said yes. He acted. He said, "Bring me jars filled with water," and His ministry began.

It may be that reading this book, reading page 73 here in chapter 5, is your moment. It may be that God is saying to you, "Your time has come. Get off the bench and get in the game. Stop thinking only of yourself, and start investing in the next generation."

You may have doubts.

"Am I mature enough?"

"Will anyone want me to be their mentor?"

"Can I really help anyone?"

If you wait, you'll be asking those same questions when you're eighty-five. And you'll have missed out on the opportunity of a lifetime . . . the chance to leave a living legacy of God followers that He used you to energize and coach.

Time Pressure Brings Focus

I've quoted Parkinson's Law for years although I've never met anyone named Parkinson. It says, "The work will expand to fill the available time." If we have twelve months to teach younger people what we've learned, then it'll take twelve months. If we have three years, it'll take three years. Time is an incredible taskmaster. When time is limited, we grab the essentials. We focus. We figure out what we're going to do and how to get it done.

The time pressure works for both the mentor and mentorees. As a mentor, I see this limited period of time, this small number of meetings, as a treasure. Scarcity increases value. I look at all the possible things I could talk about or discuss and choose the best, the areas where I'm sure I can add value, and that's what we cover. I've heard my mentorees say, "I want to get all I can get from this." So the time pressure increases focus for the mentorees as well.

Just consider the reading parts of next-generation mentoring.

A recent Harris poll showed that 38 percent of American males read less than three books per year; 9 percent read zero. In today's environment of Internet and broadcast media, fewer and fewer people read. And those who do read are reading the flavor of the day. John Grisham, Robert Ludlum, Harry Potter, wherever the buzz is . . . that's where we go.

Then consider that people who participate in next-generation mentoring groups read nine to twelve books in one year. And in next-generation mentoring, each book that's read has a clear purpose. It's connected with the goal of helping the mentorees become godly men. When they're reading *Ordering Your Private World* by Gordon MacDonald, they're reading it to learn how to manage themselves from a God-centric perspective. The books build on one another, starting with how we see God; how we see ourselves; how we relate to our wives, kids, and others. It's "on purpose" reading.

A huge piece of this program is in *how* mentorees read. I teach them to read for application. Forcing them to "net out" a book onto one page means they have to focus, to consider what the author has to say *to them*. What's the takeaway? How can this help me?

In a sense, this approach to reading is an extension of "starts now, ends then." We almost never read a book twice. Not really. We need to get what we're going to get the first time through, and being asked to "net out" the book on one page brings focus.

Just how do you "require" someone to write a net-out of a book? Come on, these are grownups! They can tell you to "pack sand" and never write down a word.

The answer is peer pressure. When a group of eight guys is gathered around with a mentor at the head of the table, you do not want to be the one who didn't do a net-out! And by requiring each guy to bring a copy of his net-out for each person in the group, a visual verification happens. If you don't have copies of your net-out for everyone, then the silent assumption is that you didn't *do* the net-out. And if you didn't do the net-out, then the silent assumption is that you didn't read the book. That then hits us where we all have a twinge of self righteousness . . . or . . . call it fairness. "If I read the book, then by George, you have to read it. It's not fair for me to have read it and for you not to."

Peer pressure.

In eight years of leading groups this way, about seven hundred books have been assigned for reading. I can recall only two instances when a mentoree has not read the book and presented his net-out. That's pretty good compliance. And I give peer pressure a lot of the credit.

The reading dimension to mentoring has one more element, the group discussion. When my group discusses a book, we share what we took away from the book—what we learned . . . what we plan to apply. We're not a book club. We don't banter around our criticism of the book or the author. It's not about that. We're about application. We're looking for principles! What did this author say that can help me become the man God wants me to be?

As we go around the table and each mentoree shares his take-aways, each person "pluses up" what the last person says. Obviously, different readers "hear" different things from the same pages. So it's always fascinating to see the diversity of application that God brings from the same book.

Through the purposeful assignment of books, the requirement for a written net-out, the discipline of having to read a book a month and being faced with the peer pressure of presenting your takeaways from each book, a reading habit gets formed.

"Reading became a habit," says Mike. "When the group ended, I immediately went looking for another good book to read and kept up with the same process of netting it out for use in the future. Reading and learning the things we did brought me closer to God, and I have kept up with that discipline since."

People get stimulated by learning and start learning on their own, and continue to learn long after the intensive period of mentoring is over. Remember, disciples are "learners and followers." Discipleship is a lifelong learning endeavor.

Jesus, the Model

Jesus did the same thing. He used the time He had for maximum learning and impact for His disciples. We don't have any record of His going deep into theology. The disciples clearly knew the Scriptures and seemed to know the prophecies that Jesus alluded to and fulfilled. He talked most about the things He knew we most needed to hear . . . money, marriage, forgiveness, relationships.

The Next Generation of the Next Generation

I was a member of Dorman High School's class of 1968 and of USC's class of 1972. We're used to being grouped this way.

An elevator fills up and those who couldn't squeeze in wait for the next car. When the class fills up for law school, some people don't get in. They either apply to another law school or wait until next year.

It's just about the only way to sequence people through a process. And while it may seem arbitrary and insensitive when applied to mentoring, it's not . . . because God's involved.

By having a defined beginning and end and knowing those dates, I can recruit future mentorees with clarity and integrity. As people approach me about mentoring, I'm able to say, "Here's the process. I ask for expressions of interest in November each year, select my guys, and then launch my group in January. If you'd like to be considered, give me your e-mail address, and I'll make sure you get invited to apply when the time comes."

Crisp. Clear. Honest.

Throughout the year I'll get e-mails and calls from young guys, inquiring about the program and wanting to find out how they can get involved. I know exactly how to set their expectations.

It's equally clear for me. I don't actually recruit people. I just live my life. And as I encounter young men who impress me—who seem to be sharp, leader types—I jot down their e-mail addresses and put them in my "future mentoree" file. Then in November I send them the same e-mail that I send to people who have approached me. They either express interest or they don't. No harm, no foul. If they respond, I know that God is involved and that we'll go to the next step. If they don't, I assume (again) that God is involved and that they're not supposed to be in my mentoring group, at least not now.

The End (The Beginning)

At the end of their mentoring year, I always feel a sense of completion even though I also feel a sadness that the time is over. Leaders and learners are always asking, "What's next?" After twelve months we've "completed the course . . . we've finished the race."

But have we?

The biggest personal surprise that's come from mentoring has been the depth of love and friendship that's developed with my mentorees. It was never my intent to get anything back from this. I wasn't looking for new friends, but God has blessed me with a plethora of incredible young friends from the guys I've mentored. And while the formal part of next-generation mentoring is over, some of the guys continue to stay in touch. It's usually those from the group within the group, those who got it and connected both with me and with God in a new and special way.

So what does that look like? What really happens after it ends? Here's my list:

- You get tons of Christmas cards . . . all with pictures of their families. (And you'll read, keep, and treasure every one—which was new for me!)
- You get calls when wives get pregnant . . . when babies are born.
- You get calls when you're sick, and guys genuinely pray for you.
- You get included in their lives. They call you when they get promoted or get a big raise. They call you when they become deacons and elders in their churches.
- You get called on when they need help. When there's a big decision in their work or when they're considering a job change, they'll call for advice.
- God uses the guys that you invest in to *love you back*.

Maybe this last one is the biggest and one I never expected. But *I know* that these guys love me. They stay in touch, take me to lunch, invite me to go to sporting events with them. They just love me, and they let me know it.

If you're a guy, stop right now and make a list of the guy friends you have *who really love you*.

If I left off the names of the guys I've mentored, mine would be a really short list. And I'm betting yours would be too.

To me this is clearly a God thing. What better gift can God give us than to put godly young people in our lives who love and care about us? Other than our wives and families, I can't think of anything.

While the intensive part of next-generation mentoring starts and ends, the love of God, lived out in the lives of the people you invest in, goes on through this life and into the next. That's pretty incredible if you ask me.

A Footnote from a Mentor

I'd be less than honest if I left this out. A little bit of joy comes when graduation happens . . . joy from having some time off.

Even though next-generation mentoring takes only one night a month, I find myself enjoying the freedom of a few weeks when I don't even think about my group. Even the best schoolteachers enjoy their summers. Having a little time between groups is cool.

The Mentoree Perspective from Richard Chancy

As I mentioned earlier, I'm a personal growth junkie. I have a thirst for knowledge that is insatiable. It seems like I can never catch up on the latest "best book you've ever read." Several years ago I set a goal for myself to read twenty-five books in a year. I was reading everything I could get my hands on. Mostly what I read was motivational, marketing, or business development. Out of curiosity I even read the classic *The Catcher in the Rye*. I was reading a minimum of an hour and a half a day and had four or five books going at any time. The problem was that my mind was going crazy trying to process so much information. I finally realized that my strategy was focused on activity rather than productivity. I was reading for distance and not to create change in myself.

So when I got a couple of months into mentoring, I was a little disappointed. Of the first three books we were assigned, I had already read two of them. Netting the books out slowed me down. I was used to burning through a book and starting another one. For me this is a major lesson in missing the point. The point was to slow down and absorb what you were reading. To actually take something away and use it. To read with a purpose.

Because our time during next-generation mentoring was so limited, everything we read was based on a crucial life topic. I can't tell you how many times one of the guys in the group said, "This was my favorite book so far" when we were netting out the books. I must have said the same thing eight or nine times. The limited amount of time made it critical to be able to go deep by using an entire month to read the material, filter out the applicable points, and complete an exercise based on the content.

The books were picked by Regi based on topics he felt would have the greatest impact on us. He selected the book from each of those areas that had the greatest affect on him.

What that meant to me was that the really hard work had been done. Here is a guy who is successful by every definition of the word who is a reader and a follower of Christ. And he is taking all the information he's pored over and is pulling out the best for us. That's huge.

As a mentor it's your responsibility to be an information filter for the guys you mentor. That may seem a little challenging at first, but, especially if you're not a reader, you'll get the hang of it over time. John Maxwell says, "Leaders are readers." It's important that you're committed to continuing to grow as well. We'll help you by giving you a recommended list to begin with in the back of this book. Also we will publish additional recommendations on our Web site along with our own net-outs to give you a feel for new books in the future.

One of my favorite mentoring books was *Decision Making and the Will of God* by Garry Friesen . . . an old book that's been reprinted many times. I learned that there is a tremendous amount of freedom inside God's will for our lives. As long as He is first in my life, I have a lot of flexibility in how I live my life. The book did a great job of explaining the boundaries that God has put before us and how to interpret them in our lives. The kicker is that I don't know if I would've read this book on my own. It was incredibly deep and started slow. (Not to mention it was 450 pages.) But I finished it and netted out the points that I'm still working through today because of the commitment I made to the group. In fact, several of the guys and I were communicating about our struggle with this book early on, and that interaction fueled my ability to keep going. And like I said, this wound up being one of the most significant books I've read.

A year may seem like a long time, but based on the topics we covered and their potential impact on my life, it really is a short period of time. We were dealing with everything from marriage and parenting to decision-making and business. Netting out the books gave me an opportunity to think through what I was reading. As I worked through the book, I could then filter the information down to what I felt was applicable for my life. Netting out is something that I'm practicing today because now I'm reading for principles . . . for change. It's important for me to be able to review what impacted me so that it moves from head knowledge to heart knowledge.

It also taught me to slow down and start reading more intentionally. Now when I read, I try to do it prayerfully so that God can speak to me no matter what I'm reading. The last book I read so profoundly affected me that I'm reading it again slowly and intentionally as I'm netting it out.

BEGIN WITH THE END IN MIND

There were really two benefits to having a begin and end date to next-generation mentoring. First, I felt like one year was a significant amount of time to dig into the process and see real change in my life. Mentoring gave me time to slow down every month and connect with the other guys. That was helpful in creating the right level of intimacy.

The second benefit was that one year was short enough to be able to make a commitment I could honor. Many things occupy space in my life without a defined end in sight. It was a comfort to know that this was a marathon and that while it *was a marathon,* there was a finish line.

6

TRUTH AT THE CORE

There are many famous mentors we all recognize.

- Socrates mentored Plato.
- Aristotle mentored Alexander the Great.
- Peter Drucker mentored Jim Collins, author of *Built to Last* and *Good to Great*.
- Andrew Carnagie mentored Charles Schwab, the famous executive and financier.
- Colonel Harland Sanders of Kentucky Fried Chicken mentored Dave Thomas, the founder of Wendy's restaurants.
- Earl Woods mentored his son, Tiger Woods.

Each of these mentors had a body of knowledge . . . *truth*, if you will . . . they had learned: philosophy, management theory, business leadership, how to create huge restaurant chains, how to play golf at the highest level. All of these mentoring relationships were based on truth. This truth was understood by the mentor at a higher, more experienced level than the mentoree. And for whatever reason, the mentor decided to share his truth with someone less experienced than himself.

A huge part of mentoring involves the effective transfer of truth from one generation to the next.

Educational, governmental, and civic leaders have been frantically pursuing mentoring as a way to transfer truth to the underprivileged . . . to boys and girls who don't have positive role models in their homes. For years we've tried to hook up people who have learned the truth required to become contributing members of society with those who don't have access to that truth in any other way.

Jesus was (and is) the ultimate mentor. And it's clear that the foundation of His life and His message was transferring truth to the next generation and all the generations that have followed. Let's look at that truth and how it played out in His life and work.

Reinforcing Historical Truth

When Jesus entered recorded history about two thousand years ago, a lot of truth was already recorded. The Old Testament law *was* the law. The Jewish people lived by it and under it. Roman occupation had created huge problems for the Jews, in many ways bringing them together as they tried to keep their religion as pure as possible in spite of living under the oppression of Rome.

Jesus was Jewish. He never tried to be un-Jewish. When questioned about some of the things He and His disciples did, He was always respectful. When He was challenged for His disciples picking grain and eating it on the Sabbath, He referenced a precedent in Jewish history when David ate the sacred bread from the temple.

When Jesus heals a leper in Luke 5:14 (NASB), He instructs him to "go and show yourself to the priest and make an offering for your cleansing, just as Moses commanded, for a testimony to them," quoting from the law in Leviticus 14:2–4.

In John 3:5, Jesus is describing being born again to Nicodemus. He says, "Unless one is born of water and the Spirit he cannot enter into the kingdom of God" (NASB). In that moment, he's referring to Ezekiel 36:25, 27 which says, "I will sprinkle clean water on you, and you will be clean; I will cleanse you from all your filthiness and from all your idols. . . . I will put My Spirit within you and cause you to walk in My statutes" (NASB).

Another time, when Jesus is warning about the sinfulness that will precede His second coming, He simply says, "Remember Lot's wife" (Luke 17:32).

He and everyone there knew what that meant. Don't sin . . . and don't even look at it. It'll get you!

Jesus had obviously learned from His forebearers, but He didn't negate the truth that God has brought to mankind through them. He tried to be clear about this in Matthew 5:17, when He said: "Do not think that I have come to abolish the Law or the Prophets; I have not come to abolish them but to fulfill them." Unfortunately, a whole lot of Jewish leaders with a whole lot to lose never believed this, and succeeded in having Him killed.

Each of us has truth that's been handed down to us from the past. My dad was a teenager when the Great Depression hit. He dropped out of school and went to work to help support his family. He never went back.

As a kid, I saw him work . . . and work . . . and work. He never thought he could take chances on better jobs because of his lack of education. So he was trapped. His boss knew he couldn't quit, so he gave him more and more work with no regard for his pay.

When he died, we found a little piece of paper in his wallet with the date that each of his children was baptized and the date that each graduated from college.

The truth I took from that? If you don't have an education, you'll always be afraid of losing your job. And you'll always doubt that you can get another one.

Later, as a dad, having seen the value that my dad had placed on getting an education, I was committed to mentoring my kids to the best education their abilities could take them to.

I gained this truth . . . not from my own experience but from the experience of someone who came before me.

Then There's What I've Learned

I've met some fathers and sons who seemed interchangeable . . . if you've seen one, you've seen the other. And that would be cool if you were Jesus, since His Dad was and is perfect.

But for the rest of us, while we learned some things from our parents and from history, most of our real learning has come from our own experience. We've had the benefit of those who've come before us, but the majority of what we know—what we live by, what guides us—comes from our own learning and experience. We're not just oracles repeating the lessons of past generations; we're experiencing life in our own unique way. We're adding to what we inherited, making it real for us in our generation.

Now we're not Jesus . . . not even close. But we see how He built on the truth He inherited. Look at how Jesus took the truth to a new level regarding forgiveness.

In an exchange with Peter, recorded in Matthew 18:21–22 (NASB), Jesus is asked about forgiveness. Peter asks, "How often shall my brother sin against me and I forgive him? Up to seven times?" (He's making reference to Genesis 4:24 where Cain was to be avenged sevenfold.) Peter was catching on. He recognized that Jesus was teaching us to replace the concept of revenge with forgiveness, but he was shocked when Jesus said, "I do not say to you, up to seven times, but up to seventy times seven" (NASB). Extreme forgiveness.

He did it again in Luke 20:34–38. The Sadducees confronted Jesus with the Old Testament provision regarding widows being remarried. Deuteronomy 25:5 had been the truth, and it had created all kinds of complicated scenarios. Who would be married to whom in heaven was one of them.

Jesus knew what the writer of Deuteronomy didn't . . . that "the sons of the resurrection"—that is, those who go to heaven—will not be married at all. They will be so enthralled with the glory of God that marriage won't even hold a candle.

And maybe the most memorable place where Jesus added new truth to the old law was when He gave us this verse: "You have heard that it was said, 'Do not commit adultery.' But I tell you that anyone who looks at a woman lustfully has already committed adultery with her in his heart" (Matt. 5:27–28).

There He is again—taking the old law . . . reinforcing it, but then raising the bar . . . moving the standard from an outward one to an inward one. Jesus is all about our hearts. He doesn't want us to live an outwardly clean life and be filthy inside. He wants purity throughout.

Over and over Jesus would share new truth. It was built on the truth of the old law, but it went further. Jesus brought new truth and new insight.

Jesus came to communicate even more of God's truth. Principles like giving, forgiveness, and compassion were concepts not always easily connected with how the Old Testament law was interpreted.

What does this mean to us as mentors? It means that you have learned a lot of truth in your life up to now. You learned from your parents, your grandparents, your teachers, your bosses, and your mentors.

You learned from the books you've read . . . and from the Bible.

You have a unique collection of truth. Over the years you've seen and heard a lot. You've discarded a lot of stuff you thought was truth but found it not to be so. More than any other source, you've learned from your mistakes . . . from the "school of hard knocks."

God has preserved you through those experiences . . . given you that truth so that you could leverage it for the benefit of others. How else can He get maximum glory from it?

I Am the Truth and the Life

The other day we received a thank-you note for a baby gift . . . not what I would typically focus on. Inside the envelope was the typical card with a nice note from the friend.

But it hit me. The message, the truth of this is in the envelope itself, not the card or even the message written on it. It was the fact that someone loved us enough, was grateful enough, to go out and buy a card, write something personal on it, find our address and write it on the front, buy and affix a stamp, and launch it through their mailbox to ours. The envelope was the real message . . . as much as or more than the contents.

And that's what Jesus was and is.

"I am the way." "I am the truth." "I am the life."

Bold but true statements. Important statements when you read the rest of that quote:

"No man comes to the Father except through me."
(John 14:6)

Jesus Himself is the truth . . . not just His teaching . . . and not just His confirmation of others' teachings.

Jesus knew who He was from Scripture. In Luke 4:18–19, He quotes from Isaiah 61:2 and Leviticus 25:10:

> The Spirit of the Lord is on me,
> because he has anointed me
> to preach good news to the poor.
>
> He has sent me to proclaim freedom for the prisoners
> and recovery of sight for the blind,
> to release the oppressed,
> to proclaim the year of the Lord's favor.

Scripture Applied in the Moment

A big part of who Jesus was came from His knowledge of Scripture. He quoted Scripture constantly, particularly when He was in trouble.

Remember when Jesus had been in the desert for forty days? He was starving, and there wasn't a McDonalds nearby. It would be a long time before Jesus could get food, no matter how badly He wanted it.

The devil came to Jesus with an offer. "The devil said to him, 'If you are the Son of God, tell this stone to become bread'" (Luke 4:3). Jesus answered the devil's tempting offer by reminding Himself (and the devil), "It is written: 'Man does not live on bread alone'" (v. 4). He was quoting Deuteronomy 8:3 which says:

> He humbled you, causing you to hunger and then feeding you with manna, which neither you nor your fathers had known, to teach you *that man does not live on bread alone but on every word that comes from the mouth of the LORD.*

Scripture wasn't just what Jesus knew . . . it was what Jesus *was.* He was able to recall a specific Scripture *in the moment* that reminded Him of God's truth and His faithfulness.

Another example, from the cross: "Jesus called out with a loud voice, 'Father, into your hands I commit my spirit.' When he had said this, he breathed his last" (Luke 23:46; also Matt. 27:50). He was quoting the first part of Psalm 31:5: "*Into your hands I commit my spirit;* redeem me, O LORD, the God of truth." His last words echoed David's.

Next-generation mentoring is about the transfer of truth . . . God's truth . . . to the next generation of leaders. And a big part of that is the memorization of Scripture by topic or theme so it can be recalled and acknowledged in the moment of need.

Communicate the Truth Learned on Your Own

Like Jesus the mentor has learned some truth on his own. Jesus got His from the Father, as they had been together since the beginning of time. We don't know, but we can guess that Jesus also learned a few things on His own, working in Joseph's carpenter shop between age twelve and age thirty. (There's that "fully human-fully God" mystery again!)

Truth comes from the mentor's life . . . just his life. Each of us is a unique creation of God, uniquely experienced, uniquely talented and gifted by God.

No one else is you.

Walt Disney once said, "The more I am like myself, the less I am like anyone else, and thus I realize my uniqueness."

The part of next-generation mentoring that transfers truth in an inexplicable way is this . . . just being who you are and letting your mentorees see "under the hood"—letting them know who you are, how you think, how you became the person you've become . . . transparency is the only way. And to hold that back is to cheat them of the best part. Just as Jesus would have cheated us had He not let us see who He really was . . . a compassionate, tender, loving, smart God-man who gave everything up for us.

"What you are thunders so loudly that I cannot hear what you say to the contrary" is a quote attributed to Ralph Waldo Emerson. Young people need to be connected with authentic, committed Christians who live their faith . . . not just talk it.

A Critical Need

Our twenty-first-century churches are just now awakening to the need for mentoring. Willow Creek Community Church, often listed among the most influential churches in America, released a study called "Reveal." The project was designed to assess just how the new church, the "seeker church" is doing. One of the resounding findings in the study is the "need for someone to interpret" the truth of Scripture to less mature believers.

In my next-generation mentoring groups, I have my guys memorize the twenty-three Scriptures that have had the most impact and utility in my life (see chart on pages 89–92).

I assign these verses two at a time. I've assigned a one-word subject to each verse so the mentorees can call up the verse by that subject.

For example, let's talk about fear. We all face fear from time to time. Some of us battle fear daily. Others less often. My wife says that I avoid fear by living in denial (which she explains is *not* a river in Egypt!).

Years ago, I memorized 2 Timothy 1:7 and labeled it as my "fear" verse. It says, "For God has not given us a spirit of fear, but of power and of love and of a sound mind" (NKJV).

I explain that verse to my mentorees this way. I can deal with something better if I know where it's coming from. Once I realized that God was not giving me the spirit of fear, then I have a pretty good hunch who is. Who other than Satan would want me to be afraid . . . paralyzed . . . neutralized with fear?

So God *has not* given me the spirit of fear. But the verse goes on to say "but" . . . a big word that says "on the other hand" or "just the opposite" . . . God *has* given me the spirit of love, power, and a sound mind.

I can deal with fear when I recognize that it's coming from a source other than God . . . a source that wants to hurt me, not help me.

Mentors Must Be Grounded in the Truth, the Word of God

They don't always have to know it by heart, but they have to *have* God's Word in their hearts. Believe it, know where to find it, trust it, never dispute it, and know how to defend it.

That's the kind of personal interpretation of Scripture that mentors can give their mentorees. I don't have a seminary degree, and I'll confess that some of my interpretations might not pass muster with some theologians. But what can't be argued is what God has shown me through His Word and its application in my life. That's what I have to give to these next-generation leaders.

Here are the Scriptures I share with my mentorees, complete with the subject I've attached to each one. If you start using the model I've used, copied from Jesus, then you'll probably want to substitute your own life verses.

Scriptures for Memorization
Next-Generation Mentoring

Priorities	But seek first his kingdom and his righteousness, and all these things will be given to you as well. (Matt. 6:33)
Purpose	I have come that they may have life, and have it to the full. (John 10:10)
Fruit	But the fruit of the Spirit is love, joy, peace, patience, kindness, goodness, faithfulness, gentleness and self control. Against such things, there is no law. (Gal. 5:22–23)
Fear	For God has not given us a spirit of fear, but of power and of love and of a sound mind. (2 Tim. 1:7 NKJV)
Humility and Gentleness	Take my yoke upon you and learn from me, for I am gentle and humble in heart, and you will find rest for your souls. (Matt. 11:29)
Peace	Peace I leave with you; my peace I give you. I do not give to you as the world gives. Do not let your hearts be troubled and do not be afraid. (John 14:27)
Decision Making	Let the peace of Christ rule in your hearts, since as members of one body you were called to peace. And be thankful. (Col. 3:15)

Contentment	I am not saying this because I am in need, for I have learned to be content whatever the circumstances. I know what it is to be in need, and I know what it is to have plenty. I have learned the secret of being content in any and every situation, whether well fed or hungry, whether living in plenty or in want. I can do everything through him who gives me strength. (Phil. 4:11–13)
Spiritual Warfare	For our struggle is not against flesh and blood, but against the rulers, against the authorities, against the powers of this dark world and against the spiritual forces of evil in the heavenly realms. (Eph. 6:12)
Decisiveness	"Simply let your 'Yes' be 'Yes,' and your 'No,' 'No'; anything beyond this comes from the evil one." (Matt. 5:37)
Wisdom	By wisdom a house is built, and by understanding it is established; and by knowledge the rooms are filled with all precious and pleasant riches. (Prov. 24:3–4 NASB)
Faith	And we know that all things work together for good to those who love God, to those who are the called according to His purpose. (Rom. 8:28 NKJV)
Teaching Your Children	Love the LORD your God with all your heart and with all your soul, and with all your strength. These commandments that I give you today are to be upon your hearts. Impress them on your children. Talk about them when you sit at home and when you walk along the road, when you lie down and when you get up. (Deut. 6:5–7)

Talk	Do not let any unwholesome talk come out of your mouths, but only what is helpful for building others up according to their needs, that it may benefit those who listen. (Eph. 4:29)
Work	Whatever you do, do your work heartily, as for the Lord rather than for men. . . . It is the Lord Christ whom you serve. (Col. 3:23–24 NASB)
Motives	All the ways of a man are clean in his own sight, but the LORD weighs the motives. (Prov. 16:2 NASB)
Thought Life	For as he thinks in his heart, so he is. (Prov. 23:7 NKJV)
Time	Be very careful, then, how you live—not as unwise but as wise, making the most of every opportunity, because the days are evil. (Eph. 5:15–16)
Honor	You husbands in the same way, live with your wives in an understanding way, as with someone weaker, since she is a woman; and show her honor as a fellow heir of the grace of life, so that your prayers will not be hindered. (1 Pet. 3:7 NASB)
Self-denial	Then Jesus said to his disciples, "If anyone would come after me, he must deny himself and take up his cross and follow me." (Matt. 16:24)
Selflessness	Husbands, love your wives, just as Christ loved the church and gave himself up for her. (Eph. 5:25)

| Prayer | Do not be anxious about anything, but in everything, by prayer and petition, with thanksgiving, present your requests to God. (Phil. 4:6) |
| Light | In the same way, let your light shine before men, that they may see your good deeds and praise your Father in heaven. (Matt. 5:16) |

Not a Complete List

Jesus didn't teach on every verse He knew, and neither should you. Jesus amplified the verses that He knew the Father wanted Him to talk about. On much of the Old Testament, Jesus was silent.

Next-generation mentoring isn't a Bible study. So don't try to make it into one or feel guilty because it isn't. Teach them the Scriptures God has used to teach you.

Scripture Applied in Retrospect

I'm going to tell you one of those "most embarrassing moment" stories about myself. This is a true story that I tell my mentorees each year to show them how memorizing Scripture by topic can be helpful if you apply it.

One of my favorite verses is Proverbs 24:3–4: "By wisdom a house is built, and by understanding it is established; and by knowledge the rooms are filled with all precious and pleasant riches" (NASB). When I assign it to my mentoring group, I explain it this way,

- Knowledge is data, information, facts, observation.
- Understanding is taking that information and putting it into context. This context may be the person you're talking about, a certain situation or circumstance; it's the background of the information that you are dealing with.
- Wisdom is knowing what to do with the information once you've considered the context.

When my son was a teenager, I was looking for something in his car and accidentally came across a pack of cigarettes. I exploded. I decided I would use the surprise tactic to get to the bottom of this smoking deal.

I dashed to his room (it was ten o'clock at night, and he was already fast asleep). I swung open the door, ran to his bedside, stuck the cigarette pack right in his face, and said "OK, buddy, what's the story here?"

He roused up, looked at me with disbelief and anger in his eyes, and said, "Those are my friend Brant's. He left them in my car. I can't believe that you were going through my car, and worse, I can't believe you would think I've been smoking. Have you forgotten who I am?"

I was humbled, stunned, and embarrassed.

I had taken knowledge (the cigarettes in my son's car) and jumped to a conclusion. Then I had acted without thinking about whether my action was wise. I just wanted the truth so I could make sure he wasn't going to become a smoker.

If I had remembered the Proverbs verse and applied it, I'd have thought, OK, *knowledge says that I've found cigarettes in my son's car.* Understanding says, "Wait a minute. My son hates smoke. He's an athlete. I need to get the full story from him before I jump to a conclusion." And then wisdom would have asked, "In what environment is he most likely to tell the truth about this?" I certainly would have come up with something more effective than my embarrassing "storm trooper/Gestapo" tactic.

That's the beauty of applied Scripture. God uses it to help you think, to respond differently . . . effectively. But it has to be in your heart, easily accessible in the moment of need.

We see Jesus using Scripture this way . . . for wisdom . . . guidance . . . never to attack people. Jesus used Scripture as a defense, not an attack.

Go and do likewise. Jesus taught us to open our mouth, and to trust the Holy Spirit to give us the words to say.

> Whenever you are arrested and brought to trial, do not worry beforehand about what to say. Just say whatever is given you at the time, for it is not you speaking, but the Holy Spirit. (Mark 13:11)

For the Holy Spirit will teach you at that time what
you should say. (Luke 12:12)

Jesus also taught us that the job of the Holy Spirit will be to
recall His (Jesus') words. So when we memorize God's truth, including Jesus' words from Scripture, we can depend on the Holy Spirit to
bring those words to mind when we need them the most.

The Mentoree Perspective from Richard Chancy

Memorizing Scripture is the centerpiece of next-generation mentoring. It ensured that I was taking some of what I was learning with
me for the long haul. A big lesson I learned was just how relevant
Scripture becomes when you memorize it by topic. The Scripture
actually becomes a part of you. It seems that there is never a day when
at least one of the twenty-three Scriptures we memorized doesn't
come to mind.

Even more amazing is how God will begin to combine what
you've memorized to guide you. Let me show you what I mean.

A few weeks ago I was riding down the road, and Matthew 11:29
came to mind: "Take my yoke upon you and learn from me, for I am
gentle and humble in heart, and you will find rest for your souls."

I really find peace in the promise of finding rest for my soul. But
on this particular day I found myself asking what it means to take His
yoke upon me. As I thought about it, another verse we memorized
came to mind: "Love the LORD your God with all your heart and
with all your soul and with all your strength. These commandments
that I give you today are to be upon your hearts. Impress them on
your children. Talk about them when you sit at home and when you
walk along the road, and when you lie down and when you get up"
(Deut. 6:5–7).

So I thought, *What do these two verses have in common?* "Take my
yoke upon you" is a direct quote from Jesus, while the Deuteronomy
verse tells me to "have these commandments upon our hearts." We
are supposed to talk about them all the time. A couple of verses
later, we're even taught to "tie them as symbols on your hands and
bind them on your foreheads. Write them on the doorframes of your
houses and on your gates" (vv. 8–9).

I don't know about you, but that sounds pretty serious to me. He's not talking in code here. Jesus verifies this sentiment in Matthew 5:17 when He says I have not come to abolish the law but to fulfill it. So I decided it would probably make sense for me to have a better idea about what these commandments were. The first commandment jumps out at me: "You shall have no other gods before me" (Deut. 5:7).

It took me a few days to get past my self-righteousness and realize the truth about the god that I tend to place before God. That god for me is all of the things I want to do to impact the kingdom of God. I had missed this for so long . . . long enough that I didn't even realize that I wasn't trying to honor Him at all. I was seeking my glory and not His. I needed to repent . . . to reconnect with God my Father. I had slipped into "pleasing God" instead of "trusting God."

Even though I've been outside of the structured environment of mentoring for some time, God is still using these memorized Scriptures to grow me, and I'm growing at an exponential rate. I'm learning so much from looking back. As I add new Scripture to my list of next-generation mentoring Scriptures, I'm looking for those that speak directly to me and the issues God is working on in my life. Now that this Scripture is inside me, I feel like it truly is a part of me and is shaping my future.

7

PRAYER AS A PRACTICE

It's like thousands of other home group environments . . . eight guys and a leader gathered around the dining room table . . . talking about God, life, and the Bible. The leader asks each guy to share his biggest need . . . his number one prayer request. He writes them down as they're spoken. Then he says, "Let's pray."

But then he disappears from sight, dropping not just to his knees but to a face-down position, completely prostrate before the Lord.

The guys don't know exactly what to do . . . how to respond. One by one they drop from their chairs and to their knees. A couple try to emulate what they see their mentor doing.

Then the mentor starts to pray. "Good evening, Father."

It's like he's hit a number on his cell phone and his dad is on the line. "Thank You for adopting me into your family. You didn't have to do that, but I'm so grateful that you did," he continues.

It's not like any prayer they've ever heard in church . . . not even like the "blessings" they've heard said around the dinner table when they were growing up. It's like a conversation . . . an authentic conversation between a father and a son. It's shockingly different.

Now I'm not telling you how to pray. That's just the way I try to pray. I try to remove as many of the church words as I can, to talk to God in authentic language about authentic stuff and in the context of our authentic relationship. In my group, I'm just letting my guys listen in to my conversation with God. I want to model authenticity in a big way because I believe we have gotten way too much like the Pharisees when it comes to prayer.

Remember when Jesus called out the Pharisees for their show-off prayers? Here's how Matthew records Jesus' words:

> And when you pray, do not be like the hypocrites, for they love to pray standing in the synagogues and on the street corners *to be seen by men.* I tell you the truth, they have received their reward in full. But when you pray, go into your room, close the door and pray to your Father, who is unseen. Then your Father, who sees what is done in secret, will reward you. And when you pray, *do not keep on babbling* like pagans, for they think they will be heard *because of their many words.* (Matt. 6:5-7, emphasis mine).

I'm authentically praying to my Father . . . nothing fake there. I try to talk to God as I would my real father . . . leaving out church words and trying to be concise and to the point. I'm praying in a way, both verbally and physically, that gives my mentorees a model, a road map . . . permission . . . to go and do the same.

Mentoring involves modeling . . . doing what you do so others can see you do it and learn. Again, Jesus shows us how.

Teach Us to Pray

Jesus must have been a fantastic pray-er. Imagine the intimacy, the love, the shared experiences, the common ground with the Father. He prayed often, going off by Himself . . . away from His followers and His mentorees.

On one key occasion, documented in Luke 11:1, Jesus had been praying. It seems that this time He had been praying with the disciples nearby because "when He finished," one of His disciples (we don't know which one) asked Him, "Teach us to pray."

I believe this disciple heard something . . . maybe saw something, that he wanted in on. Hearing Jesus pray . . . talking with His Dad . . . something incredibly compelling was going on.

Jesus responded by praying what we call the Lord's Prayer, giving us a model for how to approach the Father . . . with gratitude and humility.

We don't know if Jesus was kneeling, sitting, or face down. But because He was a devoted God follower and a student of the law, we can guess that He was in a position of reverence and submission.

Peter walked with Jesus throughout His ministry. He saw Jesus pray many times, and when he wrote his books of the Bible, he reflected the attitude that he must have seen in Jesus: "Humble yourselves, therefore, under God's mighty hand, that He may lift you up in due time" (1 Pet. 5:6).

He saw Jesus humbled and bowed down. But then he saw Him lifted up . . . first on the cross and then as He ascended into heaven. What a picture! What a contrast!

It's good for me to kneel when I pray. It reminds me that He's God and I'm not. It reminds me that I'm lower than God . . . that this isn't a conversation between buddies . . . or equals. This is humbling myself . . . acknowledging His superiority . . . putting myself below Him spiritually but also physically.

Many of the guys that I've mentored have never knelt to pray in a small group. Most have done the "kneeling bench" drill in a church sometime, but few have actually gotten down on their knees and prayed out loud with other guys.

That's what I'm trying to do . . . to break the ice . . . to use my influence as a mentor, and to use the peer pressure (and safety) of a group context to open them up to new dimensions of their faith.

One other key point: much has been written about the importance of how we see God. Do we see Him as King, as Judge, Healer . . . . that kind of thing. There's not a question to be answered here; 2 Corinthians 6:18 is clear: "I will be a Father to you, and you will be my sons."

God is my heavenly Father. That's the way I address Him; that's the way I view Him; that's the framework of our relationship; and that's the way Scripture describes Him to me. Underlying my entire approach to mentoring younger people is this truth . . . He's your

Father . . . a perfect Father. Talk to Him that way. Think of Him that way.

Jesus Was a Praying Man

You would think that a God-man wouldn't need to pray. After all, He's been with the Father from the beginning . . . participated in the creation . . . seen and experienced it all. But Jesus prayed often and for extended periods of time.

Scripture tells us that one of His longest prayer times came when He was picking His mentorees . . . His disciples. We know He would go off by Himself to pray and often. As was His practice, He would go to remote places early in the morning to be with the Father and pray.

A mentor can't be a mentor like Jesus without prayer. Here's just a short list of the things that prayer does for me as a mentor:

- Praying for my mentorees keeps me focused on them and their needs, not just my own.
- Praying for their needs gives me insight into their hearts . . . what they care about and are focused on.
- Praying for them is a way of actively loving them.

And here's a big one. *I need to pray for myself.*

It's so easy to pray for all those other people, but I also need to pray for me. God has given me influence with these guys. I need His protection, His wisdom, His courage to be who God created and saved me to be. If I fall, I damage all that He's built up in the people I've influenced. So it's important for me to stay spiritually healthy . . . on the same page with the Father and focused on the right things in my life.

Giving God the Credit for Answered Prayer

I used to keep a little whiteboard in my closet where I pray. I made two columns on it . . . one column said "Prayer Requests" and the other column said "Answers." Over time I was amazed at how many of my prayers were definitively answered . . . some positively, a lot of no's, but answered one way or the other. I mentioned this in my men's small group, and my good friend Rick asked with a smile, "Could I buy that board from you?"

I don't have the gift of intercession or anything like that. I don't even pray as often or as long as I probably should. But this little exercise taught me to keep track. I was amazed at how often God answers my prayers.

A few years later my wife and I went through the Crown Ministries course at our church and found a prayer log in the material. Just like my whiteboard, it has two columns, one for prayers and one for answers to prayers.

For my next-generation mentoring groups, I modified this log in only one significant way. I added a place to list one big prayer request . . . something with a longer term focus . . . something that a mentoree would be praying for through the entire mentoring year.

Here's what that prayer log looks like.

NGM Prayer Log

	Prayer Request(s)	Answers to Prayer
1		
2		
3		
4		
5		
6		
7		
8		
9		
10		
	My long-term prayer request:	

Grab this idea right now and start using it. You can use any sheet of paper and replicate it, or go to www.nextgenmentoring.com and download this specific form. However you choose to start, start. And start documenting as God answers your prayers.

In my groups, I give each of my eight mentorees nine copies of this form—one for themselves, one for each of the group members, and one for me, their mentor. I want to give them the opportunity to pray for one another (and for me) and to see God answer not only their prayers but also the prayers of the other guys. Answered prayer builds faith. God is answering prayers all around us for that purpose. So let's give Him the credit He deserves. It's for our benefit as well as His glory.

Listening as Well as Talking

It seems weird for us to listen to God. How do I know it's Him? Doesn't the devil counterfeit God's voice?

I confess . . . when I hear someone say, "God told me _____," I pause big time. That's not to say that God isn't still speaking. I know He is. But it's pretty hard to hear His voice and consistently identify it. And at times it's even more difficult to hear and interpret what He's saying.

In the first days after I came into a personal relationship with Jesus, a dear friend sent me a sermon series called "How to Listen to God." That series became a book by Charles Stanley, and I have never forgotten the five C's that provide a grid to help me test if what I've heard is from God. In my abbreviated fashion, here they are:

1. Is the answer/instruction consistent with Scripture? God will never direct us to do something that conflicts with His Word.
2. Will the answer challenge your faith? If the direction is the easy way out and doesn't require faith in God to execute, put a check on it.
3. Does the answer conflict with human wisdom? Often God's ways are not our ways, and what He directs us to do seems really weird to our twenty-first-century culture.

4. Does the direction clash with my fleshly nature? Sometimes God will lead me into things that require extraordinary effort . . . or self-discipline. I'll have to go against what comes naturally.
5. Will obeying God require courage? He's often giving assignments where we'll have to take risks . . . to trust Him. He's doing that to build our faith.[5]

I want my mentorees to try listening to God, to discern that "still small voice" and sort it from the messages of the world. These five questions can help me distinguish His voice from all the others.

The "Letter from God" Exercise

One activity is almost a must-do with your mentoring group. It has been the most amazing tool to help guys hear from God and learn to listen. It's called the "letter from God," and it is incredible. Credit goes to some unknown creative person or minister. I'm not smart or creative enough to come up with it . . . just utilitarian enough to grab it and share it with you!

As you prepare for this exercise, review the letters to the churches in the book of Revelation. You will see the following pattern in the letters.

Salutation. Jesus starts by calling the church by its own, unique name.

Affirmation (What God sees that is good about you). He points out positive qualities or attributes about that church. About the church at Thyatira, He says, "I know your deeds, your love and faith, your service and perseverance, . . . you are now doing more than you did at first" (Rev. 2:19). To the church at Ephesus, He says, "I know that you cannot tolerate wicked men," that "you . . . have endured hardships . . . and have not grown weary" (vv. 2–3).

Rebuke (What God holds against you). In each letter, after spelling out the things He admires about that individual church, He says, "Yet I hold this against you," and then He spells out His grievance with that specific church. To the church at Ephesus, He says, "You have forsaken your first love" (Rev. 2:4), and then goes on to point out how they had fallen away from the things they did at first.

To the church at Laodicea, He says, "You are neither cold nor hot" (Rev. 3:15), which graphically refers to His urge to "spit them out of his mouth." Get the picture?

Challenge (What God wants you to do differently). Revelation spells out what Jesus wants each church to do or to begin doing again. To Ephesus, He says, "Repent and do the things that you did at first" (Rev. 2:5). To Sardis, He says, "Remember, therefore, what you have received and heard; obey it, and repent" (Rev. 3:3).

Consequences (The results of failing to change). He spells out what will happen to the church if it doesn't respond to His rebuke. To Ephesus, He says, "If you do not repent I will come to you and remove your lampstand" (take away your influence) (Rev. 2:5). To Sardis, He says, "If you do not wake up, I will come like a thief, and you will not know at what time I will come to you" (Rev. 3:3).

Reward (God's promise if we respond and positively change). He tells the churches what the positive results of changing will be if they obey. To Ephesus, He promised, "To him who overcomes, I will give the right to eat from the tree of life" (Rev. 2:7). To Pergamum, He says, "To him who overcomes, I will give some of the hidden manna" (2:17). To Sardis, He promised, "He who overcomes will, like them, be dressed in white. I will never blot out his name from the book of life, but will acknowledge his name before my Father and his angels" (3:5).

I lead my guys in this exercise on one of our retreats. It needs plenty of time, so be sure you don't have to cut it short. I give these instructions regarding this quiet time and the assignment.

Go off somewhere by yourself, where you are around nobody. Should you run into someone, stay silent until further notice. Have some quiet time alone with God. Praise Him, acknowledge His power and His greatness, and confess anything that you need to confess. Do what you would normally do to "get on the same page" with God . . . to let His Spirit have its full place in your center.

Then take out a pen and turn to a clean sheet of paper in your journal. During the next few minutes, you are going to ask God to write a letter to you, using the pattern of the letters He wrote to the churches in Revelation.

Salutation. Write the following salutation, as writing the beginning of a letter: "Dear _____," and fill in your name. It's a letter to you!

Affirmation. Ask God, "What is it about me that pleases you?" and write down what comes to your mind. You might start a sentence by saying, "I know your deeds, that you _____," and fill in what comes to mind.

This is often the hardest piece since our low self-esteem and the guilt placed on us by the enemy makes it hard for us to hear or grasp the fact that God sees good in us. Listen carefully; you are one of His sons and daughters. He loves you very much. He put at least one spiritual gift in you when He adopted you. That can be a clue as to what He admires about you. Don't proceed until you have heard and documented His affirmation about you.

Rebuke. Begin the next section by writing, "But this thing I hold against you, that you _____," and then write down what He brings to mind. He may take you to something that you still haven't forgiven or to some job in the church that you sort of know you should volunteer for but keep putting off. It may be some besetting sin, like viewing pornography. He might convict you of constant busyness, always putting things ahead of Him and of people. Whatever He shows you, write it down.

Challenge. Ask God to show you what He would have you do differently. This is a positive action statement that will begin with an active word like *forgive* or *repent*, or *stop* _____. Ask Him to spell out for you what He wants you to do differently.

Consequences. Ask God to finish this sentence: If you don't *forgive, slow down, start tithing, break your addiction* (refer to the rebuke He showed you above), then I will _____. Ask God to show you the consequences of failing to respond to His rebuke.

Once when I did this exercise, I was convicted of staying busy all the time and never finding time to spend with God. When I asked God to show me the consequences of failing to change, I wrote, "You will become a tired and discontented old man, unable to find peace because your body won't be able to carry out the lists of 'things to do' that your mind will constantly conjure up. You will be lonely because you failed to develop the relationships that you could have had with me and with others who care about you." Quite frightening, huh!

Rewards. Conversely, ask God to show you what positive outcome He has for you if you do respond to His rebuke. Ask Him to help you finish this sentence: "If you follow my instruction and make this positive change, then _____." Ask Him to describe what will happen, what life will be like, what you will be like, what the rewards of obedience will be for you.

Then, after the six sections are completed, sign the letter, "Love, God."

This exercise can lead to incredible interaction with the Creator. On a retreat a few years ago, a fine young man named Geoff, who had been a professing Christian since childhood, came back with his letter from God and proclaimed, "Today, I interacted with God for the first time." He took almost two hours for this exercise. The rest of the group was done long before him, but there was a sense that something special was happening with Geoff and there was a supernatural patience among the group while waiting for him to finish.

Praying Together for Real

Mentoring is about using your influence with less experienced people for their good. During the mentoring year one of my goals is to encourage my guys to pray with their wives. When we come to our "graduation" night, a dinner with my guys and their wives which coincides with our last meeting, I send them off as couples to pray together.

"You may pray together every day," I say, "but you may also have never prayed together. Tonight I want you to go into another room, get down on your knees together, and pray out loud. Ask God whatever you will . . . just do it together and out loud." After a year of investment and meeting together, they aren't going to tell me "no." I have no way of requiring them to keep it going, but I have at least broken the ice by having them pray together one time.

To end the evening . . . and the year . . . my wife and I serve each couple Communion and pray privately for each couple together. We huddle up . . . the four of us . . . and pray for their marriage, their family, their future together. It's a memorable moment, and tears often show up.

Because Jesus Did

When you look at Jesus as a mentor, nothing is more visible or well documented than His commitment to prayer. We have clear pictures of Him praying for Himself and for His disciples, and prayer is the only thing we saw the disciples ask Him to teach them to do.

As you jump into mentoring like Jesus, pray. Then pray again.

Yesterday one of my mentorees called and left this message: "Regi, I know you're working on your mentoring book. I wanted to tell you about a decision I made last night. A younger guy from church has been asking me to mentor him for a while. I don't feel competent to do it. But I prayed and asked God. Before I knew it, I got my answer, called the young man and agreed to mentor him. I had been waiting for the time to start mentoring, but God showed me that there is a time to start, and now is my time."

Is now your time? Are you willing to become a mentor to the next generation? Will you do what Jesus did . . . and asked you to do? Will you pray about it?

The Mentoree Perspective from Richard Chancy

On one of our retreats, Regi had us take some time to listen to God and write a letter from God. This was a tough concept for me to put my mind around because it felt like being asked to speak for God. Most of my prayer time up to this point was focused on my "wish list" without much listening time. It turned out to be an opportunity to pay attention to what God was saying to me.

This exercise has had a lasting impact on me. Instead of trying to describe what that feels like, I thought I'd just show you what He said to me.

> *Dear Richard,*
>
> *I'm proud you've decided to do the tough work. You've opened yourself up for my review, and you are willing to examine the dark places in your heart. I'm proud of the man you've become and are becoming. My plan is for you to be fulfilled and become complete in me.*

Because of my love for you, I will continue to challenge you by testing where you find your value. Your worth is found in me alone. Do not take what is mine and pervert it in the world. If you insist on this, I cannot show you all of my ways. The path you are on is a lonely path, and it leads to every type of destruction and isolation including isolation from Kristy and Jordan . . . from your parents and family, and most of all from me. I did not create you to live alone. You will die in your loneliness long before your flesh dies. No one offers the worth I offer to you. To live in me is to be valued. Nothing else compares. My validation keeps its promise and leads to life. Your validation offers comfort, power, and control but ultimately delivers despair, loneliness, and exile.

Forget the world and find who you really are in me.

Love,
God

What I learned during my mentoring year was that having an intimate relationship with God requires two-way communication, talking to God as well as learning to listen to Him. This concept has opened a whole new level of intimacy with Christ for me. The combination of Scripture memorization and listening to God has ignited my relationship with Him.

8

TEACHING BY DOING

"We hear, we forget; we see, we remember;
we do, we understand."
—CHINESE PROVERB

Here's where mentoring is unique. A teacher can teach what he could never do himself. A coach usually coaches what he could do long ago, and in athletics it's usually long, long ago.

But mentoring involves teaching as you do something. Mentoring occurs as you're doing life together . . . being "in the moment" . . . interactive . . . like a live television show. It's real time; it's not canned, not prerecorded. It's happening right now for both the mentor and the mentoree.

Here's an example.

Steve was in my next-generation mentoring group a couple years back. Steve is an architect who, along with a partner, stepped out to start his own firm a couple of years ago.

My cell phone rang one day, and it was Steve.

"Regi, my partner was just found dead in his apartment." Steve was in shock but "in control" shock, if you know what I mean.

I asked enough questions to know that Steve was OK, that he was thinking clearly and not in a personal, emotional, or spiritual crisis.

Then I asked him about his partner's family, his parents (Kit wasn't married), brothers, and sisters. Was someone with them, attending to them personally?

Then we got to the business stuff . . . what would he tell clients who had critical projects under Kit's care? How would he get his arms around the pending work? Who would pick it up and make sure nothing bad happened? How would he deal with the employees, who would be scared out of their wits by the loss of a key contributor and leader in the firm?

We talked through all of these questions, discussed different plans of action, and came up with some next steps for Steve to take.

I've never had a business partner die unexpectedly. Steve and I were making it up on the fly.

But look at what was happening here. Because of my age and having been through several death situations in a business context, I knew what to do and the order to do things in. Steve was about to become a caregiver, and a caregiver can't give care to others unless he's *regained his own balance* from a shocking event. So my first reaction was to be sure Steve was OK . . . that he had perspective and was thinking clearly.

Second, I took him to the personal needs of the family of his partner. As Steve reached out to Kit's family, he was following the model Christ gave us. (Jesus' compassion for the family stimulated Him to bring people back from the dead!) He was also modeling the love of Christ for Kit's family and for all of his employees. In the days ahead, this compassion would be an important element because Steve would end up in negotiations with Kit's family over his estate and his ownership interest in the firm.

Finally, we got around to the business issues that needed attention.

Now here's the kicker . . . this is first and foremost why Steve called. He respects my business acumen and thought I would be a good source of advice regarding the business issues created by his partner's death. But I modeled for him a different set of priorities.

I had never dealt with this exact situation before, but I was able to both help Steve think through his next steps and at the same time teach him how to respond in a situation like this.

Jesus Taught by Doing

Prayer is the most overt example of Jesus teaching by doing. Nowhere else in the accounts of His life is Jesus directly asked to *teach* a specific thing. But be sure, as He traveled from town to town with His mentorees, a lot of what He taught them, He taught by just doing it.

When the disciples were casting out demons, they encountered one they couldn't cast out. Jesus cast out the demon Himself, then turned to the disciples and said, "This kind does not go out except by prayer and fasting" (Matt. 17:21 NKJV).

Another time the disciples came to Him with a demon-possessed man, confessing that they had failed to cast out the demon. Jesus rebuked them saying, "Oh you of little faith." Then He cast out the demon.

Let's look at some of the less obvious things Jesus taught by doing and how a next-generation mentor can go and do the same.

The Perfection of Acceptance

Jesus taught acceptance by accepting people. And He did it by accepting the most unacceptable people in His world.

He would go to the home of and dine with tax collectors and other "sinners" in the eyes of the Jewish leaders.

He would then go to the home of a Pharisee and dine. One day He was with the outsider of outsiders, and the next He was sitting with the utmost insider.

Women had a unique place in Jewish culture in Jesus' time. Many of Jesus' closest followers and supporters were women, giving us a picture of acceptance of the highest order.

Samaritans were looked down on by the Jews. Neither Jewish nor Arab, these "half-breeds" were scum to the Jews. Yet we see Jesus interacting with the Samaritan woman at the well and even praising "the good Samaritan" in one of His most familiar parables.

Sick people, especially those afflicted with diseases like leprosy, were pushed out of society altogether. Yet Jesus reached out to them, accepting them and even healing some.

Children were persona non grata in Jesus' culture. Even His disciples demonstrated a "get out of the way" mentality toward kids, but not Jesus. He invited them in, which tells us that He not only accepted them but that they felt that acceptance and wanted to hang out with Jesus.

His acceptance was universal.

It astounds people that I've never met most of the guys I choose to mentor. They've heard about next-generation mentoring from someone; they e-mail me and express an interest, but most of the time I've never met them in person.

This blind approach puts me in the position where I *must* accept each guy. I'm protected from my own biases . . . from my own judgmental spirit . . . and from the temptation to pick only guys that I naturally like. I'm picking guys that God has led me to pick, and that gives Him the maximum glory.

And throughout the mentoring year, I focus on continually accepting each guy, no matter how different he is, how differently he thinks, or how passionate he is about growing in Christ. I cannot succumb to the temptation of performance-based acceptance. That's not how God loves me, so I have to love as I am loved.

Great Mentors Are Great Listeners

Jesus listened. He was in the moment, totally focused on whoever was in front of Him. Sometimes He was listening when no one thought He was, like when He overheard James and John debating who would be the greatest.

When I'm with my group, I put my own life on hold. I want to use every available ounce of energy I have to focus on these guys . . . to hear what they're saying . . . and to understand where they're coming from. I want to teach them to do the same because my ultimate goal is for them to become mentors as well.

Several years ago my company engaged a consultant to teach us to be better listeners. He taught us four levels of listening . . . attending, content, feeling, and meaning. I understand there are even more, but these four helped me immensely and have helped my mentorees as well. Let me explain what each of these entail, and then I'll share how I try to model them and teach them to my group.

Attending. The most basic listening skill, attending has to do with our physical positioning. When I attend to one of the guys in my group, I simply face him, maintain good eye contact, and show him with my body that I'm paying attention. I'm not looking at the papers on the table in front of me. I'm not looking at my cell phone or the text message I just received. I'm not looking out the window. I'm looking at him. My hands are quiet. I'm not fidgeting . . . tapping my fingers or my foot. I'm physically focused on the person I'm listening to.

Content. Next I focus on the content of what they're saying. Word for word, I track the exact words they say, trying not to interpret or read between the lines. The content of what a person is saying is just that. It doesn't include their feelings about what they're saying, and it doesn't include your interpretation of what they're saying (or trying to say). It's just what they're saying, just as it would be typed by a court reporter.

Feeling. We are always feeling something. When we are talking, we are feeling something as we're communicating. If I'm telling about the birth of my new granddaughter, I'm feeling happy because grandkids are so much fun. Or, if I'm describing her delivery, I may be feeling relieved, as she is healthy, has all of her faculties, and both she and her mother are doing fine. We're always communicating a feeling when we talk, and the best listeners are those who can read those feelings and connect with them.

Meaning. When we combine the content of what's being said with the feeling that it's being said with, then we have meaning. We know what they said, but more important, we know what they meant. How many times have you heard someone say, "That's not what I meant!" They haven't been understood. Either their words didn't communicate what they were feeling, or the listener responded in a way that showed they didn't accurately interpret their feelings.

Understanding is the ultimate goal of a good listener and a good mentor. I really want to understand you . . . what you're saying . . . what you're feeling . . . and what you really mean by what you're saying. If I understand you, then I might be able to help you. At a minimum you'll feel my love because I listened to you. And in our twenty-first-century culture having someone listen to you well enough to understand what you're saying and how you really feel is rare.

An Exercise in Listening

To develop these skills in my mentorees, I do a simple listening workshop with them. I pair them up and have them face each other, attending to each other as described above.

Then I have one guy in each pair speak one sentence to his listening partner in the exercise. The partner is then charged with saying back to the speaker *exactly* what he said. He says, "You said," and then attempts to repeat exactly what the speaker said. It's hilarious because it's so hard to do. We're so used to cutting people off . . . to interpreting what they're saying before they finish . . . to finishing their sentences for them.

Then I reverse it, having the listener speak a sentence and his partner repeat it back word for word.

Just this simple start to this exercise causes lights to come on. Guys say things like: "Wow, listening is hard." "Listening well really takes focus." "My wife must think I'm deaf or that I don't care."

But it gets harder. Keeping the guys in pairs, I have one of them describe something from their day or week. I tell them to speak a paragraph. The assignment for the listener is to pick one word that describes the feelings of the speaker. They can only say, "You feel _____." One word. No explanation.

It's amazingly difficult, but when the listener accurately nails the feelings of the speaker, there is a huge smile and a sense of "Hey, he understood me!"

To teach them the fourth level of listening, I have one of the guys in the pair tell a brief story. Then the listener has to give a meaning response, combining the content with the feeling. It sounds something like, "You feel relieved because your grandbaby arrived healthy and in good shape."

Then I send the guys home to practice these things with their wives, at work, and with their friends. They have to report back at our next meeting what changes they saw in their relationships as a result of becoming better listeners.

Throughout the year, I attempt to model these listening skills. If I can help guys become better listeners, they'll be more loving people and more like Jesus. Ultimately they'll be better mentors too.

On Time and Prepared

Years ago I had hired my first consultant to recruit a vice president of sales for our company. At the end of the project, he asked me what he could have done to improve his performance or serve me better. I mentioned a couple of things, and then I asked him, "What could I have done to be a better client?"

He said, "Do you really want to know? I mean *really* want to know?"

I knew something was coming, but there was no turning back at this point. So I said, "Yes, give it to me straight!"

He said: "Regi, you were late for every meeting we had. Sometimes, I would wait outside your office while you talked to others on the phone, not only finishing up conversations but also initiating new ones. The way you disrespected our appointment times communicated that you disrespected me."

I was stunned. If I were in biblical times, I would have torn my clothes and covered myself in ashes. What he described was not the man or the business person I want to be, not to mention the way my selfishness and disrespect for him and his time reflected on me as a Christ follower. Jesus cared for people . . . He would never dis them the way I had dissed this consultant (who was also a good friend!).

From that day I've passionately pursued being on time for everything. And when my mentorees are involved, I break my neck to be on time.

I'm teaching them the importance of being on time by being on time.

Serving

Throughout the year I'm teaching my guys to serve by serving them. When they arrive for our meetings, everything is ready. Copies are made, books are bought, refreshments are out—whatever it takes. I try to put them and their needs ahead of my own.

During the mentoring year I go to each guy's workplace, pick him up, and take him to lunch. I buy.

On our retreats I look for every opportunity to serve. I make everything as easy as I can for them because I want them to feel what it's like when someone you look up to serves you. I know of no better way to teach service than to serve.

Remember the powerful moment when Jesus stood, removed His outer garment, wrapped a towel around His waist, and washed His disciples' feet? In that culture washing feet was the lowest, nastiest job. But Jesus did it to model serving in a radical, emotional, physical way. Afterward He added meaning to His act, explaining how love is about serving.

> "Now that I, your Lord and Teacher, have washed your feet, you also should wash one another's feet. I have set you an example that you should do as I have done for you. I tell you the truth, no servant is greater than his master, nor is a messenger greater than the one who sent him. Now that you know these things, you will be blessed if you do them." (John 13:14–17).

Even in Dying

Jesus taught us how to die as He did it Himself. He knew the end was near. He was able to pray . . . to talk to His Father . . . to prepare Himself mentally and spiritually.

Death is something we have to do all by ourselves. Jesus went to the garden to pray, taking His disciples with Him. But He left them to "watch here," going on alone to talk to God. We know He asked if there was any other way . . . something any of us might pray in the same situation. He struggled with what was coming, praying with such intensity that His sweat was bloody. But after He was prayed up, He took it on with courage and resolve.

He stood innocent in front of Jewish and Roman authorities yet said nothing. He never cried or begged . . . never defending Himself. He hung in maximum pain and thought of His mother, making sure that John would care for her after He was gone. He reached out to the criminals on the crosses beside Him. And then He asked His Father to forgive the people who were doing Him in. Incredible!

But the most impressive thing that Jesus taught us in how He died is the way He trusted God all the way through, especially in the end. Quoting Scripture, Jesus said, "Into your hands, I commit my spirit" (Luke 23:46). He asked for another way out. He suffered excruciating pain, and He felt abandoned—all natural reactions to what He was experiencing.

Yet with confidence, when He came to the end, He said, "Father, I'm at the jumping off place. I'm letting go of this life and depending on you to catch me."

Years ago my three-year-old son showed blind faith as he would climb up on things and jump into my arms. With reckless abandon he'd leap into the air, never doubting that I'd be there to catch him. Because Jesus demonstrated that kind of faith, and it was obviously rewarded by His having life after this life, we can face death with that same kind of faith and confidence.

We all do better when someone is watching. As you embrace this mentoring challenge, you'll realize that you're teaching by doing, that you're doing life all the time, and that your mentorees are watching. I'm teaching my mentorees how to love their wives by how I love my wife . . . how to love their kids by how I love mine. I'm teaching them how to love and serve the church by how I love and serve my church. And in the end I'll teach them how to transition from this life to the next . . . by how I do it myself. I hope I can be as cool as Jesus.

The Mentoree Perspective from Richard Chancy

Early on in the mentoring year, Regi set the pace for us by sharing his story. He told us about the career path he was on and all the attention he was getting from the brass at AT&T. He was a young man in the company but was rubbing elbows with the guys at the top. It sounded like he had already grabbed the brass ring of life until he started telling us about what most people didn't see.

Miriam, his wife, was all but an afterthought. Moving up the ladder was moving her farther down the priority list, and the same was true for his children. The story of those years is a heavy one, but the real message is the current story, what you see when you see them together now.

The first time I met Miriam was when all of the mentorees and their wives met at Regi's for dinner during the third month of mentoring. We had dinner and got to know one another a little better, and then the wives and husbands split up into different rooms. Regi took the guys as usual, and Miriam took the ladies. We did our normal session while Miriam had a great conversation with the girls.

Miriam is clearly a part of Regi's mission, not just a prayer partner but an active part of what he is doing. He had invited her into the adventure, and she was in it with him. She listened to my Kristy and the other young wives . . . she showed that she understood their pain and angst. She encouraged them in their family life and their faith.

In just the last few months, I've been asking myself how Kristy and I can team up like that. We lead a small group together, and we've started splitting the men and women up and talking about real stuff. The results in the group have been really amazing. We've gone to a whole new level. It's hard to describe what it feels like. It is an amazing feeling to have her with me in serving these people.

A few weeks ago Kristy and I had dinner with Regi and Miriam. When we got in the car after dinner, we talked about how, even though they've been married for thirty-nine years, they seem like they are still dating. They are so in tune with each other, and they genuinely enjoy each other. That's what I want from a mentor: just live your life, live it well to God's glory. But let me watch!

9

THE CONTEXT OF
WHEREVER

A friend of mine spoke profoundly when he said mentoring is about content, community, and context. Content has always been a "biggie" because people who mentor in the intentional fashion will always want a curriculum. In the secular world, mentoring is built around a specific purpose. The curriculum would be around that purpose. In the Christian world, there's no recognized content for mentoring beside the Bible itself.

Community is a new element to mentoring, and it becomes a meaningful element when you mentor in a group environment.

But what about context? What is it? Why is it important?

The Where of Mentoring

When I think of mentoring, I see two guys having coffee or lunch. It's always in a restaurant . . . always around food or drink because that makes starting conversation and keeping it going easier.

They've become friends. Conversation flows naturally, but most of it centers around the younger man's life . . . his issues, his opportunities, his future.

Traditionally the mentoring relationship is almost always initiated by the mentoree. He has something he wants . . . a felt need . . . for guidance, wisdom, advice, or help. Most often these conversations get started around job stuff. The younger man needs advice or access to the older man's network of contacts. Sometimes it's a crisis at home . . . a breech with a wife or child; and the less experienced person wants to confide in someone who's "been there, done that."

Since he's on his own agenda, the mentoree suggests a location that's convenient for the mentor . . . both in time and place. After all, he's the one who's getting the help. Why shouldn't he make it easy on the guy who's giving it?

Now, is this a type of mentoring? Yes. Is it what Jesus did? No.

Jesus *initiated* the mentoring relationship with His disciples. He approached them. He chose them.

In Mark 3:13–14, we're told that "Jesus went up on a mountainside and called to him those he wanted, and they came to him. He appointed twelve—designating them apostles—that they might be with him and that he might send them out to preach."

Everything about what He did was about *His agenda*, not theirs. Jesus didn't worry about being an inconvenience to His mentorees. He knew that He was giving them the *chance of a lifetime* by allowing them to follow and learn from Him.

Later on, Jesus would tell them, "Blessed are the eyes that see what you see. For I tell you that many prophets and kings wanted to see what you see but did not see it, and to hear what you hear but did not hear it" (Luke 10:23–24).

Remember when Jesus told the man that he had to give up everything if he wanted to experience the kingdom of God? Peter (as usual) spoke up on behalf of the disciples and reminded Jesus, "We've given up everything." These are not the words of men who are in something for their own agendas. Sure, they hoped Jesus would appoint Himself as earthly king and they'd be well-placed in that hierarchy. But the point is that Jesus invited them to follow Him, and they did. They left their businesses, their wives (at least in Peter's case), and their families to take Jesus up on His offer to become "fishers of men."

And when they said yes to His offer, they dropped their nets and hit the highway . . . literally. Unlike the rabbis who had passed them over for discipleship, Jesus was itinerant. He traveled constantly. Jesus took His mentorees into *His* context . . . for *His* purposes.

Had the disciples gone the traditional route and studied under a traditional rabbi, they'd have been in their hometowns, living in their communities, and doing life in the traditional way. They'd have learned their lessons in the synagogue and taught there as well. Their lives would have been insulated from outsiders . . . people who were sick or deformed . . . Samaritans, tax collectors, and sinners. They'd have lived in a "holy huddle." And no one would have ever heard of them.

But instead, they followed Jesus. Miles and miles they walked. Jesus talked. They listened. Jesus healed; they watched. Jesus did miracles. They marveled. And it was all done "along the way."

Taking It to the Streets

Here's a partial list of places where Jesus mentored His disciples:

- along the road
- in the garden
- at the well
- at Peter's house
- in the synagogue
- on the mountains
- on the water
- by the sea

When you mentor younger people, you'll find yourself in all kinds of places. While my monthly meetings take place at my home, I visit each guy's workplace once during the mentoring year. And yes, there are other one-on-one meetings for breakfast or lunch. I've attended church with mentorees. I've gone to football games and special events; played volleyball and golf; camped out; gone boating, fly-fishing, waterskiing, and jet skiing—you name it. One of my mentorees was married in my backyard. Many times in those environments, questions come up, and teachable moments present themselves. But most of the time I spend with my mentorees, I spend at my home.

At Home, Exposed

When mentorees come to my home, they get an up-close and personal look inside my life. They meet my wife. They would meet my kids if they weren't grown and gone. They see my house, my yard, my furniture. They even meet my dog.

They see my mementos . . . my trophies if you will. And those trophies show them what's really important to me, just as yours show what's important to you.

The walls of my rec room are what's been called a "heritage wall." One of my guys' lovely wife, Rachael, designed it for me. When you walk in the door and turn left, you start our life story with pictures of my parents and Miriam's parents. Then there are our baby pictures . . . pictures of us as kids, and so forth. As you go around the room in chronological order, there are logos of all the businesses that I have worked in or helped start. Then come pictures of our kids, starting as babies all the way through their wedding pictures, and then grand-kids. The stories of our lives are told in those pictures. When I take my guys on the tour, they see how I've spent my time. Sure, there's a smattering of travel pictures, whitewater rafting on vacation, etc. But the wall is covered with two themes, and only two . . . family and work. That's not to put myself on any kind of pedestal. It's just real.

If you love to travel, then your trophies may be stuff from the places you've been. Or if you're an avid golfer or fisherman, then your trophies will say so. I believe our trophies give our guys permission to have interests, to enjoy the life God has given them, and to do so guilt free.

John Piper tells how he experienced the great "coming together" as he calls it.

> What was life about? What was it for? Why do I exist? Why am I here? To be happy? Or to glorify God? Unspoken for years, there was in me the feeling that these two were at odds. Either you glorify God or you pursue happiness. One seemed absolutely right, the other seemed absolutely inevitable. And that was why I was so confused and frustrated for so long.
>
> God created me—and you—to live with a single, all-embracing, all-transforming passion—namely, a

passion to glorify God by enjoying and displaying his supreme excellence in all the spheres of life.[6]

Enjoying and displaying. Both for God's glory.

In the context of our lives, we enjoy God and display His love and the God life for the men that we mentor.

The Stuff of Life

We have my mentoring group guys and their wives over for dinner . . . once in the spring and once in the fall. Both husbands and wives get to see how Miriam and I function as a team when we're entertaining sixteen guests in our home. They watch how we interact, how we care for each other and for them. Like it or not, we're role models in this context. And modeling love and respect makes a huge impression on these young couples.

Jesus used the everyday things and events of life to make His points. When He was confronted by the Jewish leaders about the oppressive Roman tax, He used the Roman coin to illustrate His answer: "Give to Caesar what is Caesar's and to God what is God's" (Matt. 22:21). How cool was that . . . to use the image of Caesar on the coin to make the point of ownership . . . Caesar owned the earthly kingdom, but if we accept His ownership, we can belong to God . . . become a part of His family and His kingdom—because we're made in *His* image and are owned by Him.

He did it again when confronted with paying the temple tax. He sent a fisherman (Peter) to fish, this time with a line instead of a net. And Peter caught the specific fish that God willed, enabling Jesus and Peter to pay their temple tax (see Matt. 17:25–27).

Jesus used fig trees, loaves and fishes, spit—all kinds of regular things—to make points. As modern-day mentors, we need to use the stuff of life to point our protégés toward the Christ-led life.

Forgiveness is a huge issue for all of us. Over and over guys come with their boss stories . . . how their bosses do incredibly thoughtless and insensitive things. "What do I do? Do I just pretend it didn't happen? What's my response supposed to be?"

And as we sit around the dining room table, I and the group members will ask questions, call up relevant Scriptures; and before long a path emerges. "I have to tell him what I think . . . how I feel . . . and then forgive him and move on." A wise course of action, charted by the guy who has the most to gain or lose, but with a little help from his friends . . . in his context.

What to Say (or Not to Say) at a Funeral

Recently a friend lost his father after a long, debilitating illness. Chris, one of my mentorees knew the older man . . . had met him through a Bible study group a couple of years back. We decided to drive to the funeral together, and as we entered the hall and took our place in the receiving line, Chris turned to me with some consternation and said, "What do you say at these things?"

Haven't you had that uneasy feeling? We're sad that he's gone, but at the same time we knew it was inevitable. He had suffered for a long time . . . his family was exhausted from trying to care for him. It was his time.

"Nothing," I replied. "Don't say anything."

"Nothing?" he asked quizzically.

"Nothing. Look each member of the family in the eye, say, 'I'm sorry for your loss.' Hug them. And then just be there."

I had learned this years ago when my good friend Rick lost his wife to brain cancer. I stood at the funeral home and watched as hundreds of people came by. One by one they blabbered words and more words. It made me want to cry for Rick. He'd just lost his wife, and now he's got to hear people say things like, "She really looks good," after viewing her body in the casket, and, "I know you're happy she's in a better place." The man just lost the love of his life. He wants her back! The better place can wait!

What Rick needed was the presence of people who cared for him and his kids. No words can express the pain and loss he was feeling, so why try to do the impossible . . . to say what can't be said? Just stay quiet. Be gentle, caring, and concerned. But keep your mouth shut.

We can't teach the next generation these things in a classroom. We have to go through things with them. We have to do life together and teach them along the way.

You see, life doesn't happen in church. Church can prepare us for life, and it can provide us shelter when the storms of life start beating on us. But life happens at home, at work, on vacation, in our neighborhoods. If we're going to share a "piece of our map" with the next generation, for their benefit, then we must be out on the road with them, doing life together. The lessons get taught in the context of everyday life, in everyday situations, through the wisdom of God planted and nurtured in the life of one of His more mature kids.

Speaking of Kids

Of all the contexts God uses to teach us, I believe children are one of His favorite tools. And it shouldn't surprise us since He explains Himself to us through the Father-Son paradigm. Our parents had a profound impact on us as we grew up . . . either commission or omission. So we inherently understand what it's like to be a child depending on his dad for approval, courage, guidance, and even discipline.

But in all my years of mentoring, I've found few of my mentorees have awesome dads. Their dads have been absent, abusive, critical, and selfish (just like me before I surrendered to Jesus).

The result are men who've missed the joy of growing up feeling totally loved. In his book *The Way of the Wild Heart*, John Eldridge says it this way:

> There are many, many men who never knew the happiness and security of being the Beloved Son, and therefore never really got to be a boy in fullness and freedom. They might be angry; they might be uncertain of themselves; they may have looked to the woman for love, or to another man. They may be overachievers, or dropouts. They are all around, and they still need to know. The boy within needs to be raised from the depths of the soul where he has hidden or been banished so that the man can "get on with his life." The boy inside must be raised, raised to the status of Beloved Son.[7]

Eldridge goes on to say that our growth as men is stunted by the absence of this "beloved son" stage and that we have to go back and experience that stage if we are to grow to maturity. We do that by learning to let God "father" us . . . by grasping the fact that God *is* our Father, our perfect Father. And that He wants to love us . . . to "father" us all the days of our lives. We are His beloved sons!

That may be the most important part of context . . . to realize that no matter where you are or what you're doing, you have a Mentor. He's always available. He has the wisdom of the universe at the tip of His tongue. And He cares about you . . . and me.

I did the father switch many years ago. Thankfully, I released my earthly father from his job as father (and my expectations of what he was supposed to do and be) well before he died. That release, pardon, forgiveness—whatever you want to call it—allowed us to heal our relationship and be friends until the day he died.

I didn't lose a father when I "fired" him as my dad; I gained one. Because I "hired" my heavenly Father to take his place. My heavenly Father has been awesome. He's yet to let me down. He's there for me, always available and always accepting and loving. He'll give me guidance if I ask Him, but He'll also stay out of my way and let me "have my head" if I choose.

When the next group of mentorees comes parading into my dining room, it won't be long before we'll start digging into their relationships with their fathers. And when they begin to see their fathers clearly, they can begin to see where *they* are headed as fathers. Our natural inclination is to parent the way that we were parented. So we have to make intentional choices to parent differently and then to live those choices out. I made some of those choices and chose wisely. In some cases I was able to live out my choices with great outcomes. In others I didn't stick to my guns as well and don't feel as good about what I did. And in yet others I just didn't know what to do as a dad.

My goal is to share with my mentorees what I did right and what I'd do differently. I confess both with as much clarity and transparency as I can. As a mentor the only way good can come from the mistakes I've made is if two or more people get to learn from my painful errors.

As we go through the year together, kid issues come up, and they're often brought to the group with a big "I need help" tag on them. As I listen and guide the discussion, I remind the guys that they have a perfect Father. Ask Him what He would have you do. He's the role model and a far better mentor than I can ever be. If I can share what I did (or didn't do) in a similar situation, I will . . . if I'm sure it will help them with their issue.

Mentoring is not counseling. There are people who are trained to do that. When a mentoree is bringing an issue to the group, there is more to the story than he's telling (and more than he even knows, in all likelihood). So it's dangerous to start shoveling out advice and platitudes when you don't even have all the facts.

But as the mentor, if I can have the maturity to point them to the Father, then I've done my job. Because He'll be there to mentor them long after I've passed on . . . when my "context of wherever" has become my "context of forever."

The Mentoree Perspective from Richard Chancy

A few months back Regi agreed to meet me for lunch to discuss a career change I was making. I'd been with the same organization for six years and really felt like it was time to do something else. I'd already had the conversation with my boss, who's also a great friend, and he was very encouraging.

When I sat down with Regi, I put in front of him my résumé and three different opportunities I was considering. My goal was for Regi to guide me in finding some clarity on what was next for me.

The first opportunity would allow me to continue to work closely with churches and pastors, which I really enjoy. I have a passion for helping people grow through the local church. The second opportunity would place me back in corporate America where I had spent most of my career and would open new opportunities to connect with guys outside the faith. The third opportunity was 100 percent ministry oriented. This one would put me in a brand-new arena and challenge all of my strengths and weaknesses.

I was leaning toward the first opportunity, but I went into the conversation with Regi with a high degree of objectivity, not trying to sell him on any particular path. I wanted him to be able to speak freely without feeling like he needed to "turn the *Titanic*" if what he saw was different from what I was thinking.

As we began to dig in, he asked me several questions, but one really struck me. He asked, "Tell me about your best day ever at your current job."

That is a great question. As a side note, Regi has trained himself to ask the really good questions in the right way. They are thought provoking and neutral, meaning they don't lead . . . they just make you stop and think. That is a great quality in a mentor.

Back to the story. As I thought about my best day, I began to describe it to Regi. I told him about the day I had an opportunity to work with the staff of a church to help them determine who they are as a body of believers. The process required a lot of wrestling among the staff. The best thing about this group was that they had seen what happens when there isn't a strong vision . . . they were wide open for determining theirs. There were several great interactions . . . you could see the walls coming down . . . a common vision was emerging for their church. It was truly incredible to be a part of it.

Regi was processing all that I was saying. Then he began to ask me questions to clarify what it was that "blew my hair back" that day. He then asked me which, if any, of the opportunities I was considering would allow me to *experience that kind of joy* every day.

He had given me a lot to think about, and that conversation changed the direction of what I chose to do. The neat thing about it was how he came into my world not with both guns blazing but more like a tennis coach. I hit the balls over the net, and he simply changed the angle of the return with great questions.

As far as what I chose to do career wise, I guess you're reading it. I spend all my days trying to help churches create mentoring groups, and I love it!

10

A MUTUAL COMMITMENT

"Without question, the unique factor in next-generation mentoring is commitment."

I've been leading next-generation mentoring groups for more than eight years. In all, there have been 768 opportunities for my mentorees to be late for a meeting or not to show up at all (eight guys per group, twelve meetings per year, eight years = 768 meeting opportunities).

In eight years there have been nine absences and seven tardies. That means people have shown up and shown up on time 99 percent of the time. Isn't that amazing?

And remember, I have no authority over these mentorees. We're all volunteers. They pay nothing to participate and receive no compensation for attending or being on time.

I've run companies where I had *authority* over my employees . . . controlled their incomes and bonuses . . . even their job security . . . and I've never had anything close to that kind of attendance and timeliness record.

So what is it? Am I that good? Do I threaten them with knives and guns?

You Have Not Because You Ask Not

In reality it's as simple as setting clear expectations up front and then following through on them. I make it important for everyone to attend every meeting. I sell them on the benefit of that and then reinforce it whenever I have to.

Earlier I described the situation when a mentoree called at 5:00 p.m. on the day of our meeting. "Regi, I just can't make it tonight. My boss, the CEO, has us in a planning session, and we're not going to be finished until 10:00 or 11:00 tonight. What should I do?"

Here's the moment of truth . . . for me and for Bryan. Do I do the typical, nice, Christian thing and let him off the hook? If I do, I'm communicating that attending isn't really all that important. Remember, he signed a covenant, and it said, "You will have to make some tough choices" in order to attend every meeting and be on time.

My response?

"Bryan, you made a covenant with me and this group."

"Yeah, but this could be life and death for me at work. My CEO is standing right here . . . will you talk to him?" pleads Bryan.

"No, I don't need to talk to him. You do. You need to explain the position he's put you in, and then you need to make a decision. I'll love you either way, and you won't be kicked out of the group if you don't show up. But pray about this and make a wise decision. Good-bye." And that's where I left him.

Bryan, the other mentorees, you, me . . . we all have to make tough decisions all the time. Maybe not as visible as this one, but we're constantly deciding which of our commitments we're going to break.

Andy Stanley nails this dilemma in his powerful little book *Choosing to Cheat.* His premise is that we can never meet everyone's expectations . . . that we have to "cheat" somewhere . . . disappoint someone . . . shortchange something.

This was a good field exercise for Bryan, to face his mentor and his boss and decide which commitment he would honor. And he chose to stay at work, much to the chagrin of his group. They totally broke on him at the next meeting . . . and not in a lighthearted way. They were seriously rebuking him for his decision. I didn't say anything. But later I had the chance to meet Bryan's boss in person. He thanked me for my investment in Bryan and gained a lot of respect for Bryan by how he handled the decision-making process.

Each year one of the new mentorees forgets that he lives in Atlanta, Georgia, where there are significant traffic issues every day, and shows up late. I sit quietly until that last person is seated. I then have them open the journal that I've placed in front of them, and I instruct them to write this down: "In Atlanta, traffic is always an issue but rarely an excuse."

I then give them the speech I told you about earlier, about how devastated I was when I saw how being late communicated disrespect to the people who were waiting for me, and how my five minutes of tardiness is actually forty-five minutes of wasted time if it holds up a group (five minutes for nine people equals forty-five minutes).

That is usually the last tardy of the year.

If someone is late after that, I communicate my displeasure in nonverbal ways. I never laugh it off . . . I'm intentional about keeping a standard . . . an expectation . . . that everyone be on time.

High Commitment Is Attractive

The fastest growing religions in the world, in fact the only growing religions in the world, are those that demand something from their followers. Islam, particularly radical Islam, is a vivid example, calling its young followers to complete commitment of everything up to and including death.

Mormons rigorously give, avoid sinful habits, and spend extended stints as missionaries around the world. In America the more conservative the denomination, the faster the growth rate. Where people are asked to do something, not to do something, to give up something, those are the growing faiths. It's only valuable if it costs you something.

We shouldn't be surprised by this. It's a principle Jesus taught clearly. "For where your treasure is, there your heart will be also" (Matt. 6:21).

Our freedom, our time, our money . . . whatever we treasure . . . when we give it up for something, our hearts will follow. When our involvement is optional . . . when we can go or not go, take it or leave it, then our hearts won't be in it.

So we know that watering things down, reducing the level of commitment required, and taking away accountability reduces the numbers long-term. Why do we continue to head in this direction?

The Tyranny of Numbers

America has become all about the numbers, measurable outcomes.

Two pastors were overheard at lunch:

> "How many are you running in Sunday school?"

> "We're running about 350. How about you?"

> "Oh, we're off a little. I guess it was that sermon on sin. I think we'll bounce back up now that we're talking about grace."

If the numbers aren't headed in the right direction, something has to be wrong. We are driven by numbers throughout our society. As my CFO used to say, "Numbers are like hostages . . . torture them long enough, and they'll tell you whatever you want to hear."

In managing case sales of Coke or production quotas at Honda, numbers are essential and can't be diminished. But in creating Christ followers, it's dangerous.

Typically, we want to be inclusive to the max. We want as many people to attend as we can possibly get because we think that shows success. And in certain businesses, like selling seats in a seminar at $500 a head, that may be true. But in disciple making it might not be.

The church in America has fallen victim to this numbers game by doing whatever it takes to get people in the seats. We think that if we give homework, fewer people will show up. If we hold people accountable for doing the homework, we might embarrass them, and they won't come back. And worse, they'll tell others, and then we have a bigger problem. Preachers get run off for such as this.

We consistently compromise the quality of the program or of the learning experience in order to appease the peripheral participant. By trying to maximize the numbers, we minimize the effectiveness.

A growing number of young believers want to make a difference for the kingdom. They want to learn . . . to grow. They're willing to make sacrifices to make that happen . . . to make commitments and live up to them. They are tired of the lukewarm, wishy-washy, show up if you feel like it, "only if the sun is shining" kind of involvement that the church so often facilitates.

Born of a Sense of Fairness

When I began leading mentoring groups, I thought about this a lot. I asked: "Why would I commit to something for a year, do some preparation, open up my home and my life, only to have guys show up when they feel like it? That isn't fair! If I'm going to commit, they should too. And their commitment should mean something."

So I made up a covenant.

I'm not going to bore you with a discourse about covenants and contracts. Just know that making a covenant was a big deal in Old Testament times, and people today innately sense that a covenant is a serious commitment. Let me show you the covenant that I came up with.

Next-Generation Mentoring Group Covenant

We are hereby making a covenant commitment to the following:

1. I understand that I will be given tough, off-target feedback. I will do all within my power to receive this feedback in love and to learn from it. I will avoid defensiveness, knowing that when I defend, I lose the opportunity to learn. I am committing to being open to examine myself—my personality, my past, my habits, my anger, and my responses to people. I want to learn. I want to change, to be more like Jesus Christ in every fiber of my being.

2. I understand that I am committing to attending every
   meeting and retreat, being there on time, and having my
   work done. No exceptions unless *providentially* hindered.
   I understand and agree that I will have to say no to
   important things in order to meet this commitment,
   and I am willing to do so. We will lay out our schedule
   for the year at our first meeting. I will manage my other
   commitments around the dates that are selected for next-
   generation mentoring meetings and retreats.
3. I will "finish the course." I understand that both Regi and
   the group will make a significant investment in me. Because
   it is unfair and disrespectful to them, I am committing to
   the entire year and will finish well.
4. I understand that this mentoring process is based on Jesus
   Christ, His message, and His plan for our lives. I understand
   that I will be asked to be totally vulnerable about my
   relationship with Christ, for the purpose of growing in my
   faith.
5. I, Regi, pledge to give the same level of commitment,
   dedication, and energy to you. I will visit with each of you
   in your workplace sometime during the year, I will have you
   and your wives over for two events during the year, and
   I will attempt to teach and lead from a humble, transparent,
   and loving heart.
6. I further covenant that, at some point, when the Lord lets
   me know that I am ready, I will pick eight guys and lead a
   group like this myself.

Now that's pretty serious. Each candidate for mentoring is given
this covenant before he is selected for the group. And they're told,
"Hey, if you can't live up to this, then don't commit." You'll be taking
a spot that someone who *can* and *will* commit could use.

Next-generation mentoring isn't about breadth; it's about depth.
It's not about how many we can mentor; it's about taking the ones we
can mentor deep into the faith. So it's fine if someone can't make this
covenant.

Each of the provisions in the covenant deserve some kind of
explanation.

1. Feedback and Introspection. I want each mentoree to know that mentoring requires honesty. Jesus didn't mince words with His disciples. He called it just as He saw it. A good mentor has to be honest, not so he can beat on his chest, but because it's what helps the mentoree the most. Nowhere else in our world can we get direct, honest, well-intentioned feedback on ourselves. In addition I want to invest in learners . . . people who are open to examining themselves . . . who want to grow and be all that God has made them to be.

2. Attendance and Timeliness. You can't develop intimacy and trust in a group that never really becomes a group. When attendance is sporadic, you don't remember who's heard what. Everyone quickly ends up on a different page. It's not like a Bible study where you just catch up your homework and you're good to go. This is people sharing their hearts, telling their life stories, dealing with issues that it's likely others in the group will be dealing with sooner or later. So you just can't be constantly starting over and doing it over. And as I earlier described, when eight people are waiting for that one that's late, every minute wasted is multiplied by nine. So five minutes late means forty-five minutes of wasted time. That's unacceptable.

3. Finishing. If I'm committing to a whole year, then why shouldn't every person in the group make the same commitment? If one or seven drop out, I won't abandon my commitment, so why not demand the same commitment from the mentorees? In eight years I've had three people move during the year, and in each case they commuted back to attend the sessions and retreat without missing a single one. Last year, Jonathan Johnson commuted nine hours each way from Slidel, Louisiana, to Atlanta, to complete the mentoring year and live up to the mentoring group covenant.

4. Christ Centered. I make no bones about it. Jesus Christ isn't a priority in my life; He *is* my life. And my purpose in mentoring these younger men is to show them what that Christ-centered life is all about. No surprises. No excuses.

5. The Mentor's Commitment. My covenant is with God, but I spell out some of it here for the mentorees to see. I want them to hold me accountable for delivering on my promises. During the third year of leading these groups, my mother-in-law was at the point of death. My wife and I were at her bedside in another state. At 7:05 p.m., my cell phone rang, and the caller ID was from my home telephone in Atlanta. Could I be calling myself? No, it was my mentoring group. I had failed to let them know of the situation, and they had come to my house, broken in, and were sitting around the table, waiting for me to show up. Needless to say, I was both embarrassed and humbled. But I was also proud that my guys took their commitment so seriously. I orchestrated the meeting by phone. I got it started, and they took it from there. Other than that, I've never missed a meeting, a commitment, or an assignment.

6. **Multiplication.** In order for me to agree to invest in a mentoree, he has to agree to invest in the next generation. Call it "pay it forward" if you will. I call it multiplication. More on that in the next chapter.

Jesus Set the Bar

We don't know how Jesus created commitment within His mentorees. We know that He had a large number of disciples . . . we know how He sent out seventy in one instance. Sometimes hundreds were following Him, and sometimes four or five thousand were sitting at His feet, listening to Him teach. To have been picked to be an apostle, an insider, one of the closest of the close, must have been pretty special.

The one human quality we can always depend on is selfish interest. And while we know these guys felt special to be chosen by this "rock star" rabbi, other motives were at play. At least some of the disciples may have had a vision of earthly power, of status, maybe even wealth. They followed with a sense of awe as they saw this ordinary carpenter's son heal people, bring people back from the dead, and speak wisdom that was astounding. But in their minds was an earthly kingdom . . . and possible freedom from Rome . . . and they stood to be important players in that deal if it happened.

This becomes obvious at the end when Jesus was arrested and ultimately crucified. His mentorees scattered. The fishermen returned to their nets. They were still getting together, trying to figure out exactly what happened. Their dreams were dashed, and their mission was *over* as far as they knew. But when Jesus came back to life, everything changed. His teachings came alive just as He did. They saw the "temple rebuilt in three days" and knew its significance.

After He ascended forty days later, they began to tell their unabridged story of what they had seen and heard. In the end their commitment to Jesus and to telling His story cost all of them except John their lives.

Jesus wasn't there to hold them accountable . . . to call them out when they were late or when they drifted off course. But they had the Holy Spirit and maturity, just as we do today. The Holy Spirit convicts, guides, and comforts. And their maturity enabled them to know what was important . . . when to speak and when to stay quiet . . . and how to communicate Jesus' message in the most effective way.

Attentiveness to God . . . maturity in our relationship with Him . . . that's what next-generation mentoring is all about.

You can't get there without commitment. But the growth that can come when a mentor and his mentorees make a covenant and keep it is pretty amazing. God will honor that commitment and show up. He promised.

The Mentoree Perspective from Richard Chancy

During our first meeting we set our schedule for the entire year. We scheduled every session as well as two weekend retreats. The spring retreat would be spent at a mountain cabin close to our home, but the fall retreat was to be at a house on the coast, about a six-hour drive from Atlanta.

A couple months into the year, Regi realized that he needed to switch the retreat locations due to some construction going on at the beach house. So the beach retreat would have to be in the spring and the mountain retreat in the fall. Since we would be driving so far, the beach retreat would require an extra day . . . four days versus three. That meant we would need to leave one day earlier for the retreat . . . not that big of a deal unless your ten-year anniversary was on that day!

I e-mailed Regi to let him know that I'd need to make other arrangements, and he responded in a way that was sympathetic while at the same time not letting me off the hook. Over the next couple of weeks I really struggled with this. I had made a commitment to the group, but I hadn't committed to spending my tenth anniversary with a bunch of hairy guys.

My wife, Kristy, was a little shocked when I told her about the situation, but she was completely understanding and, as usual, gave me a lot of grace to do what I needed to do. So this wasn't really about her expectations of me. It was purely about my commitments conflicting.

In the end I decided to take our anniversary day off from work, spend the whole day with Kristy, and then leave with the guys in the late afternoon for the retreat.

The real fireworks started up for me a few months after the retreat. One of the men in the group had moved and was doing this unbelievable nine-hour drive back for each meeting. Somehow, something was said like, "No one else has really had to sacrifice much for this!" That really hit a nerve with me, and I refreshed everyone's memory about my anniversary sacrifice. The irony is how I turned a free trip to the beach into a sacrifice. So when Regi asked each of us to give a speech on the fall retreat, I chose commitment as my topic. I was going to have the final word as to the true meaning of commitment, which would be recorded for posterity. It's said, "We teach what we most need to learn." Well, here's my lesson about commitment.

Commitment is one of the words I've used a lot. Talking about commitment without a full understanding of its meaning is like using a scalpel to spread peanut butter. You can try it, but when you use it, it'll bite you. It really benefited me to take some time to slow down and consider what this word means.

The dictionary defines *commitment* as "an engagement or obligation that restricts freedom of action." This definition tells only one side of the commitment story. If I'm giving up something in my commitment, surely there is a quid pro quo. There's a "what's in it for me?" in there as well. There has to be!

When I commit to something, there is a reason behind it that directly or indirectly benefits me. In most cases, if I'm truthful, I'm looking for plenty of benefit with little cost of freedom. What I gained by understanding commitment is that in most cases I make decisions and not commitments.

When I joined Regi's group, he did as much as he could up front to let us know what would be involved. In reality though, all I saw was the potential upside for me. I was going to have the opportunity to spend a season with a guy who has really been around the block.

I knew this could be a turning point for me and could only imagine the doors that could be opened from this experience. I committed, but I hadn't made a commitment where I had considered the known sacrifice much less the potential of unforeseen sacrifice. I simply made a decision based on the benefit to me. I only considered the upside.

Because of this thought process, I've had a tendency to over-commit. I give people a false sense of my willingness to be involved in something; and when two of those commitments come into conflict, the relationships involved may be damaged.

Since my mentoring experience, I try to weigh carefully the true cost when I have opportunities in front of me. I want to make sure I have done a good job of understanding just what is being asked of me and how it will affect my family and the other obligations I have.

Just the other day, I was asked to play in a men's softball league. I really enjoy being with this group of guys; but as I think through the commitments I've made to my family as well as to a local ministry, the decision to decline was easy.

Making a commitment to a season of mentoring will cost you something. Make it carefully. But know that the freedom you limit through this commitment is not a cost . . . it's an investment. And the return on this investment . . . the payback . . . is still coming in as I walk through life a better man.

11

PAY IT FORWARD

According to Wikipedia, the expression "pay it forward" is used to describe the concept of third-party beneficiary in which a creditor offers the debtor the option of paying the debt forward to a third person instead of paying it back. Debt and payments can be monetary or by good deeds. In sociology, this concept is called "generalized reciprocity" or "generalized exchange." A related transaction, which starts with a gift instead of a loan, is alternative giving.

The concept was described by Benjamin Franklin, in a letter to Benjamin Webb dated April 22, 1784:

> I do not pretend to give such a Sum; I only lend it to you. When you [. . .] meet with another honest Man in similar Distress, you must pay me by lending this Sum to him; enjoining him to discharge the Debt by a like operation, when he shall be able, and shall meet with another opportunity. I hope it may thus go thro' many hands, before it meets with a Knave that will stop its Progress. This is a trick of mine for doing a deal of good with a little money.

The term "pay it forward" was coined, or at least popularized, by Robert A. Heinlein in his book *Between Planets*, published in 1951:

> The banker reached into the folds of his gown, pulled out a single credit note. "But eat first—a full belly steadies the judgment. Do me the honor of accepting this as our welcome to the newcomer."
>
> His pride said no; his stomach said YES! Don took it and said, "Uh, thanks! That's awfully kind of you. I'll pay it back, first chance."
>
> "Instead, pay it forward to some other brother who needs it."

We connect the term "pay it forward" with the 2000 Warner Brothers film by that name staring Kevin Spacey, Helen Hunt, and Haley Joel Osment.

Osment plays a twelve-year-old boy who comes up with the idea of doing three good deeds for others in repayment of a good deed that one receives. Such good deeds should be things that the other person cannot accomplish on their own. In this way, the need to help one another can spread exponentially through society, creating a social movement with the goal of making the world a better place.[8]

Mentoring as Jesus did is the ultimate "pay it forward" challenge. Why?

Gifts Can't Be Repaid

First and foremost, we cannot repay God for what He's done for us. The gift of salvation, the gift of forgiveness, the gift of eternal life, the gift of His presence in our lives . . . these are priceless assets He gave us. We owe nothing. The debt was cancelled; the price paid by Jesus at the cross.

But what about the people who led us to Jesus? Can't we pay them back? The answer there is no for a couple of different reasons.

We have to recognize that their deal was with God, not with us. They were simply being obedient to Him . . . doing what He asked them to do. God did the leading, the loving, the saving, and even the discipling. He just used His team . . . His children, to allow them to participate in the fun.

Second, the people who led you and me to Christ, if they were rightly motivated, don't want to be paid back. The way you pay them back is to pay it forward.

In *About My Father's Business* I described my relationship with Craig Callaway and how he became a Christian after twelve years of conversations. Craig is one of my best friends now, and he's now having discussions with a work colleague named Jeff. He's sharing books with him, answering his questions, and helping Jeff on his spiritual journey toward Jesus.

Nothing could give me more pleasure. No payback gift could be as meaningful as seeing my friend Craig trying to "pay it forward" to Jeff. He couldn't pay me back anyway . . . I only did what God asked me to do. As I became friends with Craig, I couldn't possibly be his true friend without caring about his spiritual direction and destination. Over time I tried to help him with his questions and move him toward a relationship with Christ. No pressure. No rush. Just love and acceptance. The same that he's now expressing to Jeff.

Mentoring Is Paying It Forward

In the movie *Pay It Forward*, each good deed is paid forward with three additional good deeds. Imagine if this were times eight instead of three. And what if the people doing the "paying forward" were paying forward good deeds with eternal impact?

As I said in the beginning of this book, the "pay it forward," or multiplication model that Jesus used, creates astounding numbers. When you think of teaching a Sunday school class of eight people for seven years, you've impacted fifty-six people. But when each person I teach "pays it forward" by teaching eight others, and they "pay it forward" by teaching eight more, before long, you have a movement. That's what Jesus created and what he intended for us to continue and expand.

It's been said, and I don't know by whom, that you haven't created a disciple until your disciple has created a disciple. That seems to be a pretty high standard, at least by today's norms. That principle would raise the bar considerably, meaning that until the person I've invested in is deep enough in his faith and motivated enough to infect others, my job as a disciple maker isn't done.

But how can I affect what someone else is or isn't going to do? How can I affect not just the next generation but the generation after that?

I once heard Bruce Wilkinson address this question. Bruce put three chairs on the platform, and he used the examples of David, Solomon, and Rehoboam.

In chair number one, he put David. We all know that David was "a man after [God's] own heart" (Acts 13:22). Now, David messed up with Bathsheba and her husband . . . that's for sure. And he was *passionate* about God in every dimension of his life throughout his life. But was he intentional and passionate about passing his faith on to the next generation?

Chair number two represented Solomon. Solomon was a God follower but not nearly as passionate as his father, David. He started out fine, but as I read Ecclesiastes, I hear the voice of a man who has lost his way. His behavior showed it as he compromised God's instructions, marrying an Egyptian (Pharaoh's daughter) in disobedience to God and ultimately becoming corrupt and perverted. He had faith, but he was smart on his own, and his faith was in *moderation*. He seems to have grasped little of what was passed on from his father.

Solomon's son, Rehoboam, was represented by chair number three. The faith that Solomon handed down to Rehoboam was confusing to him. It sort of meant something but sort of didn't. When Rehoboam assumed the kingdom, his faith was *meaningless*. His unwillingness to take counsel led to the division of Israel into two countries and ultimately to the loss of the kingdom altogether.

The point?

We're going to hand off our faith to our children first and then to others. That faith will be what it is . . . if we're passionate, they'll know it. If we're moderately committed to Jesus, what we pass on will be moderate at best and most likely meaningless. There is no faking it. People are smart. They know the difference between genuine, authentic faith and shallow, public faith. I love the clarity of C. S. Lewis's statement: "Christianity, if false, is of no importance, and if true, of infinite importance. The only thing it cannot be is moderately important."

But just having an intense faith and intimate relationship with Christ won't ensure that it's "paid forward" to the next generation. We need intentionality.

Intentionality—My New Favorite Word

We do such a small percentage of the things we think we're going to do. As the saying goes, "The road to hell is filled with good intentions." With technology I now have vivid evidence of my recalcitrance. I make my task list, pull it over to my calendar, and then watch the list of undone tasks pile higher and higher. When it comes to interactions with people, it's worse. Those interactions tend to be even more spurious and haphazard.

The mentoring approach I've described in this book is all about intentionality. It removes my excuses for not investing in future generations. By picking a small group of people, laying out a schedule of meetings, assigning books to be read and Scriptures to be memorized, I've created an intentional plan for influencing this small group of people for Christ.

Everything in the program is intentional. Each Scripture is intentionally connected to a life issue. Each book is selected to address an area of our life and walk with God; from decision making, to priority setting, to spiritual warfare, to marriage and fatherhood, each read is intentional. Visiting each guy at his office is intentional.

Playing games with the guys on retreats is intentional. Paying for their food is intentional. Cooking and cleaning up after them is intentional. Serving them Communion is intentional; praying with them is intentional; and then graduating them and sending them out to pay it forward is clearly intentional. At every step, the intention is to help them become the man that God created them to be.

Maturity Is Essential

The basic premise of mentoring is to show mentorees not just how to do something but also how to be something. Hopefully, through the time we spend in the mentoring year, my mentorees will have seen some of Jesus in me and be well down the road toward replicating it in their own lives.

Early in this book I shared what I thought were the attributes of the best mentors. But I want to bring those attributes to the fore once again.

Maturity. A good mentor must have maturity. It's essential. It's nonnegotiable.

Dictionary.com says that *maturity* is a "state or quality of being fully grown or developed." Spiritually, none of us will ever *feel* like we're there. But being "fully grown" from a spiritual perspective is not that hard to ascertain. Thankfully, we don't have to guess about what *fully grown* means. Our God and Father has spelled it out for us clearly.

Faith. A mature Christ follower is connected with a body of believers and has a rock-solid faith in Jesus Christ. He uses the "body" (i.e., the church), and invests in it to build up the younger ones. And why? "To prepare God's people for works of service, so that the body of Christ may be built up until we all reach unity in the faith and in the knowledge of the Son of God and become mature, attaining to the whole measure of the fullness of Christ" (Eph. 4:12–13).

It's a cycle. We mentor so the body can be built up—so that there will be unity, knowledge of Jesus, and spiritual maturity to the max. The mature then perform works of service, which include mentoring the next generation. And so on.

Good-hearted. A mature Christ follower has a good heart. As Jesus taught using the parable of the seeds, He described the mature believer. "But the seed on good soil stands for those with a noble and good heart, who hear the word, retain it, and by persevering produce a crop" (Luke 8:15).

Confident. A mature Christ follower who is ready to be a disciple maker has confidence. He's not cocky . . . he doesn't know all the answers. But he knows the God who does and how to find those answers through prayer and through God's Word. Check this out: "Epaphras, who is one of you and a servant of Christ Jesus, sends greetings. He is always wrestling in prayer for you, that you may stand firm in all the will of God, mature and fully assured" (Col. 4:12).

Dependent on God. While maturity involves confidence, it's not self-confidence. It's confidence in a dependable God. "All of us who are mature should take such a view of things. And if on some point you think differently, that too God will make clear to you" (Phil. 3:15).

Wisdom. A wise person knows the difference between right and wrong and chooses right regardless of the consequences. Wisdom comes from gaining knowledge and applying it, gaining experience that can be applied to the next situations. Maturity comes with experience. "But solid food is for the mature, who by constant use have trained themselves to distinguish good from evil" (Heb. 5:14).

Perseverance. To be mature one has to have faced challenges and overcome them. You have to have lived long enough to know that things worth having are worth both working for and waiting for. "Perseverance must finish its work so that you may be mature and complete, not lacking anything" (James 1:4).

When Will I Be Ready to Mentor?

If you read these last words and know in your heart that all of these words describe you, then you're ready to mentor. Isn't it cool how God gives us the answers to important questions?

One of the mistakes I've made in my mentoring is in leading my guys to believe that they need to wait until they're over forty . . . "when they know something." That's a mistake and one that I'm in the process of fixing.

I mentored Brian a couple of years ago. He was one of those in that "inner circle" that I spoke about earlier . . . the "group within the group." Brian called the other day to tell me that he's going to begin mentoring. He's not yet forty, but he's ready.

"Regi," Brian said, "I used to think there was *the* time to start mentoring. Now I think there is *a* time to start, and my time is now." When I think of Brian and ask those questions, I think he's right.

> *Does he have a rock-solid faith in Jesus?* Yes.
>
> *Is he connected and committed to a church . . . a body of believers?* Yes.
>
> *Is he good-hearted?* Absolutely. . . . I've watched him live out his faith.
>
> *Is he confident?* Yes.
>
> *Is he dependent on God?* Yes, and in a healthy way.
>
> *Is he wise?* Yes.
>
> *Will he persevere?* Yes, he's a "stay and play" guy . . . not a quitter.

So there you have it. A mentor is launched. And God is smiling.

But Where Do I Start?

Another question that constantly surfaces is who to mentor, where to start, what age group?

As I was driving along the expressway recently, it came to me. The answer lies in one word . . . confidence. A mentor has to have complete confidence that he will know most of the questions that he'll be asked. Yep, it's knowing the questions that will be coming at him that gives him the confidence to put himself into a mentoring role. No one knows all the answers. But having lived through a season of life and having dealt with the questions that arise gives us the confidence to walk through it with younger ones.

So here's an approach.

Think backward.

Think about the seasons of life that you've already come through, working from where you are right now back as far as you have to. When you get to the season where you have complete confidence in your ability to mentor, to know the questions that people within that age frame will have (and some of the answers), then you've discovered your place to start.

Clay was in my last next-generation mentoring group. He's pretty mature for a twenty-eight-year-old. He's been married for four years . . . no kids yet . . . but a pretty "together" young man. He wants to mentor. And he wants to start now.

Looking back at the seasons of life he's been through, he sees:

- Young married guy just out of college; first jobs, no kids.
- College guy
- High school senior, getting ready to go off to college

Bingo!

Clay knows the questions high school seniors face. He's been there. He "navigated those waters" successfully ten years ago. And now he's had those years to digest his experience . . . to press meaning into the decisions he made, and to see how those decisions played out in college, in marriage, and in his entry into the "work world."

He has complete confidence in his ability to mentor high school seniors. He's handpicked his first group and is off to a wonderful start.

Sure there's more to it. He prayed. He sought "the peace of Christ" about his decision. He talked with his wife. He sought the counsel of two other mentors before he launched into this. But he figured out where to start by looking back.

Take a few minutes and think through your "age frames." Where are you now? What age frame or "season" of life did you come through before the one you're in now? What was the one before that? Keep thinking back through those age frames, one by one, until you get back to one where you think, *Hey, now I* know *something about that one!* That age frame, the one where you know the questions (and some of the answers), that's where you're going to feel completely confident as a mentor. And that's probably where you should start.

The Commitment to Replicate

Whether you buy into my eleven practices of the world's greatest mentor or not, I hope you will at least buy into the "pay it forward" principle and make it a habit. Never agree to mentor someone unless he agrees to mentor someone else down the road. And as I've said, I like the numbers when one person pays it forward times eight.

Jesus was never foggy about replicating. From His first call to His first mentorees, He made clear that His kingdom was about making them "fishers of men." It was about more than leading the disciples to faith. They obviously had demonstrated their faith just by dropping their nets and taking that first step. If Jesus was just looking for them to believe, He could have immediately said, "OK, OK, it's clear that you guys believe in Me. You've shown you're willing to stop what you're doing and follow Me. So just go back to work and have a nice day. Your faith has saved you."

But that wasn't His deal. He wanted them to experience the joy of being a part of the redemptive process . . . of becoming "fishers of men." And they did.

The "bookend" of Jesus' earthly mentoring relationship with His mentorees ended as it began with the call to "go and make disciples." Pretty consistent challenge I'd say.

And they did as He asked, traveling thousands of miles, telling the stories of Jesus—not so much what He taught as what they saw. Ultimately most of them were killed for telling what they saw their mentor do. That's commitment.

My mentorees covenant to mentor at least one group of eight in the future. I believe that many will become lifers and lead many groups. It's hard to stop when you experience the joy of seeing your mentorees gain the whole-life maturity that Scripture talks about and knowing that you played a key role in helping them toward that maturity.

The Real Mentor

As I've walked you through the practices of mentoring the way Jesus mentored, it's my hope and prayer that you're inspired to become a mentor as well. It will be one of the most fulfilling, "on purpose," things you will ever do in your lifetime. You can't fail so long as your motives are pure and you follow the principles I've laid out for you.

But there is one more point to make . . . maybe the most important one of all when it comes to mentoring.

God is the mentor. Always.

He wants to be the perfect mentor to every single one of His children. As we "sit at the feet" of older, wiser people, He is loving on us, teaching us, coaching us.

When we're doing the same for our mentorees, He is doing the work, teaching the lessons, giving the guidance. It's all about Him.

Just as we can't "save" anyone, we can't mentor anyone either. We love them, pray for them, give them our best advice and help, but God brings the increase, and thus God gets the credit.

After all, He is the world's greatest mentor.

The Mentoree Perspective from Richard Chancy

As I wrap this up, I thought it would be a great exercise for me to list just a few of the life benefits I've gained through this intense season of mentoring.

MARRIAGE

First, I truly believe that my relationship with my wife, Kristy, is much better. A couple of years ago, I would have described my marriage as good. But as Jim Collins said, "Good is the enemy of great." My "good" marriage was stagnant in so many ways. Kristy and I didn't realize just how flat things had become. This past year I learned that intimacy with God is directly proportional to intimacy with her. She is the main vehicle through which God has chosen to love me.

PARENTING

I stopped expecting my six-year-old to act like a thirty-six-year-old. We read a great book on raising children, and one of the main takeaways for me was that I was expecting Jordan to act like I do. The real release in that revelation is just how fun a six-year-old is when given the grace to be six. She's awesome, and God has begun to use her to show me just how much He loves me.

During the last year God has taught me so much about these two girls and how my relationship with them is so critical to my relationship with Him. They are teaching me every day the meaning of the words *love, grace,* and *acceptance.*

MY RELATIONSHIP WITH GOD

In the last year I've learned just what it means to begin to trust God with my life. I've seen how much I have lived in the fear of the unknown. I memorized a verse on fear: "For God has not given us a spirit of fear, but of power and of love and of a sound mind" (2 Tim. 1:7 NKJV). He's taught me that when I can't trust a person or a situation, I can always put my trust in Him.

Learning to listen to Him has been life changing. He is constantly guiding me and reminding me of the way He has designed me to live . . . how much pleasure I get when I put Him first. My thirst for relationship with Him expands and grows as I learn more about and live in His grace.

Living Out of Who God Made Me to Be

God revealed to me what He designed me for early during the year of mentoring. I learned that "I exist to serve by igniting passion in God's people." As I begin to understand just what that means, I'm beginning to see opportunities to live it out. When I wake up in the morning, it's often the first thing that I think of. Many times during conversations with people I love, God has me thinking of how I can ignite the passion God has placed within this person.

These four areas are a large part of the adventure God has called me to live. Just as the Scripture we memorized is impacting me in many ways I don't yet understand, I'm sure that I'm not yet aware of many benefits to this process. Several major directional changes came from being mentored, but many more small "one degree" changes will show up in my life years down the road. I thank God for all of them.

ABOUT THE AUTHOR

Regi Campbell is a businessman and entrepreneur. He has been involved in thirteen start-up companies, most with an emphasis in technology. He holds an MBA from the Moore School of Business at the University of South Carolina. He has served as an elder with Andy Stanley at North Point Community Church, one of America's fastest growing and most influential churches. Regi and his wife, Miriam, have two adult children and live in Atlanta, Georgia.

APPENDIX

Books to Consider in Next-generation Mentoring

Bell, Rob. *Velvet Elvis: Repainting the Christian Faith.* Grand Rapids, MI: Zondervan, 2006.

Blanchard, Kenneth H. and Spencer Johnson. *The One Minute Manager.* New York, NY: William Morrow, 1982.

Campbell, Regi. *About My Father's Business: Taking Your Faith to Work.* Sisters, OR: Multnomah, 2005.

Campbell, Ross. *How to Really Love Your Child.* Colorado Springs, CO: Cook Communications, 2004.

Chapman, Gary. *The Five Love Languages: How to Express Heartfelt Commitment to Your Mate (Men's Edition).* Chicago, IL: Northfield Publishing, 2004.

DeHaan, Dan. *The God You Can Know.* Chicago, IL: Moody, 2001.

Eggerichs, Emerson. *Love & Respect: The Love She Most Desires; The Respect He Desperately Needs.* Nashville, TN: Thomas Nelson, 2004.

Eldridge, John. *Wild at Heart: Discovering the Secret of a Man's Soul.* Nashville, TN: Thomas Nelson, 2001.

Farrel, Bill and Pam. *Men Are like Waffles; Women Are like Spaghetti: Understanding and Delighting in Your Differences.* Eugene, OR: Harvest House, 2007.

Friesen, Gary. *Decision Making and the Will of God: A Biblical Alternative to the Traditional View.* Sisters, OR: Multnomah, 2004.

George, Bob. *Classic Christianity: Life's Too Short to Miss the Real Thing.* Eugene, OR: Harvest House, 2000.

McCarthy, Kevin. *The On-Purpose Person: Making Your Life Make Sense: A Modern Parable.* Bedford, Ohio, OH: Pinion Press, 2001.

McDonald, Gordon. *Ordering Your Private World.* Nashville, TN: Thomas Nelson, 2007.

Peretti, Frank. *This Present Darkness.* Wheaton, IL: Crossway Books, 2003.

Smalley, Gary and John Trent. *The Hidden Value of a Man: Created to Lead, Empowered to Succeed.* Carol Stream, IL: Living Books, 2005.

Stanley, Andy. *Louder Than Words: The Power of Uncompromised Living.* Sisters, OR: Multnomah, 2004.

Stanley, Andy. *Next Generation Leader: 5 Essentials for Those Who Will Shape the Future.* Sisters, OR: Multnomah, 2003.

Stanley, Charles. *How to Listen to God.* Nashville, TN: Thomas Nelson, 2002.

Thrall, Bill, Bruce McNicol, and John Lynch. *TrueFaced (Revised Edition).* Colorado Springs, CO: NavPress Publishing Group, 2004.

Young, William. *The Shack.* Newbury Park, CA: Windblown Media, 2008.

NOTES

1. John Piper, *Don't Waste Your Life* (Wheaton, IL: Crossway Books, 2003), 45–46.
2. Owen W. Linzmayer, *Apple Confidential: The Real Story of Apple Computer* (San Francisco, CA: No Starch Press, 1999), 122.
3. Jim Collins quoting Peter Drucker, www.kaush.com/archives/000605.html.
4. John MacArthur, *Twelve Ordinary Men* (Nashville, TN: W Publishing Group, 2002), 78.
5. Charles F. Stanley, *How to Listen to God* (Nashville, TN: Thomas Nelson, 1985), 49–54.
6. John Piper, *Don't Waste Your Life* (Wheaton, IL: Crossway Books, 2003), 31.
7. John Eldridge, *The Way of the Wild Heart* (Nashville, TN: Thomas Nelson, 2006), 60.
8. See www.Wikipedia.com.

For more information about mentoring and how to launch next generation mentoring in your church, visit . . .

www.nextgenmentoring.com